Basic
English Grammar

by

Bonnie L. Walker

AGS®
American Guidance Service, Inc.
Circle Pines, Minnesota 55014-1796

About the Author

Bonnie L. Walker has taught for sixteen years in junior and senior high schools and in college. She holds a Ph.D. degree in curriculum theory and educational media from the University of Maryland and has also earned a bachelor's of art degree with honors in English. She studied psycholinguistics at the University of Illinois Graduate School. She is the author of several textbooks, workbooks, learning packages, and sound filmstrips in written expression, grammar, composition, and usage.

Staff

Barbara Pokrinchak, Ed.D., Executive Editor
M. E. Criste, Editorial Consultant
Beth C. Hornung, Editor
Norm Myers, Design Services

Printed in the United States of America.

ISBN: 0-88671-472-9 (Previously ISBN: 0-86601-958-8)

Order Number: 80010

A 0 9 8 7 6 5 4 3

CONTENTS

Preface

The English language is exciting and ever-changing. Every day people create new words that help them to express their ideas. Grammar is the study of the basic rules of our language — the way we use words in sentences. Grammar is the glue that holds the language together. Over the years grammar changes slowly.

Basic English Grammar has two parts. Part One is about grammar and usage. Students will learn about each of the eight parts of speech. Part Two is about sentence structure. Students will learn about each type of sentence in spoken English. They will also learn about verbals and their usage in sentences.

Organization of the Text

Each part of the book is organized into Chapters, Lessons, and Activities. The grammar rules and their uses in sentences are represented together in each lesson to help students understand the rules and their practical application to the patterns of written and spoken English. Each lesson includes a variety of activities designed to help students identify parts of speech, apply grammar rules, and check their writing for mistakes. This final activity helps students to recognize and to correct errors in usage.

All chapters begin with an overview of the topic and Chapter Warm-Up exercises, which may be used as diagnostic activities or pretests. Each lesson focuses on the development of one important subtopic or concept related to the main idea. Within each lesson, the rules are presented with accompanying activities. Review activities are incorporated at the end of each lesson and at the end of chapters.

More Practice

Approximately 400 activities appear in this textbook. For more practice, there is an accompanying workbook with 64 pages of activities that follow the topics in *Basic English Grammar*. There are also computer software programs and Blackline Masters to help you practice identifying parts of speech and grammar rules.

The Teacher's Guide

The Teacher's Guide to the textbook includes numerous writing and group activities to provide more help with each topic. For each lesson, the Guide lists any difficult vocabulary included. There are also lesson summaries, objectives, recommendations for instructional sequence, follow-up exercises, and answers to exercises.

PART I

GRAMMAR AND USAGE

What do you really know about grammar?

Grammar is the study of language. When we study grammar, we are learning to speak and to write effectively. The purpose of grammar is to help us to communicate our ideas.

- Grammar includes the way words are arranged in a sentence.
- Grammar includes the rules for spelling, punctuation, and capitalization.
- Grammar also includes rules about usage.

The study of grammar includes the way we use words in sentences. When we write, we must express complete ideas. Often we know when we hear a mistake in usage even when we do not know the exact rule.

When we speak, we use pauses and gestures to make our meaning clear. We also emphasize some words more than others. We can talk in a loud or a soft voice. However, when we write, we must use punctuation and capitalization to help us make our meaning clearer.

The following activities will help you to test your knowledge of grammar so that you can review what you still need to learn.

Activity A. Here are some groups of words that do not make sense. Rearrange the words on your paper so that they have meaning.

1. Graduated from high school in June Jack.
2. Went Manuel on a vacation.
3. To a new band listened Mike.

Activity B.   Decide whether these sentences are questions or statements. Add the correct end punctuation.

1. Do you want something to eat
2. Jack stopped at the store and bought sodas
3. Is Cathy going to the beach this summer

Activity C.   Each of these sentences has a mistake. The mistake may be spelling, capitalization, or punctuation. Find the mistake. Write the sentences correctly on your own paper.

1. Brian lookd out of the window.
2. "Is this a good day for fishing," he wondered.
3. Last wednesday he caught several fish.
4. he caught an enormous catfish.
5. Brian decided to ask his friend joe.
6. He new they would have a good time.

Activity D.   Read each sentence. Find the usage mistake. Then, write the sentence correctly.

1. Me and Charlie enjoy going to concerts.
2. Jackie and Frank have already went to the movies.
3. He changed the oil in his car hisself.
4. Gail don't like to eat spinach.
5. Us boys are going to play softball tonight.
6. That story doesn't make no sense.
7. Howard walked up to me and gives me an apple.

PARTS OF SPEECH

The English language has thousands of words. All of these words can be put into eight main groups. These groups are called parts of speech and are important for you to know.

In this book you will study all eight parts of speech. You will understand your language better. Then, it will be easier to use your language when you speak and when you write.

Nouns: Words that name people, places, things, and ideas.
Alex and his **girlfriend** enjoy **concerts**.

Pronouns: Words that replace nouns.
Everyone likes **him** very much.

Adjectives: Words that describe nouns or pronouns.
The last concert was **expensive**.

Verbs: Words that express action or a state of being in a sentence.
Alex **looked** at used cars all day.
My knee **is** hurt.

Adverbs: Words that tell about the action. They can tell how, when, where, or how much.
He drove his new car **carefully**.

Prepositions: Words that show relationships between a noun and the rest of the sentence.
Jack drove **over** the bumpy road.

Conjunctions: Words that connect sentences or parts of a sentence.
Bill **and** Ann bought the tickets.

Interjections: Words that express feelings.
Ouch! You stepped on my foot.

Every word in a sentence is a certain part of speech. Many words can be more than one part of speech. You must see the word in a sentence to know how it is used. For example, many words can be either nouns or adjectives.

> Noun: I like to play **softball**.
> Adjective: We went to a **softball** game.

A word can also be used as either a noun or a verb. You must read the sentence to be sure. A word that names someone or something is a noun. A word that expresses the action is a verb.

> Verb: They **race** their cars every weekend.
> Noun: The **race** started at three o'clock.

Activity E.   Read each sentence. What part of speech is the boldfaced word? Write your answer on your own paper.

1. Billy McGregor is a **baseball** player.
2. He enjoys playing **baseball** very much.
3. Billy **plays** second base.
4. He is a good hitter **and** fielder.
5. Billy is **unusually** quick.
6. After high school **he** tried out for a team.
7. Billy plays **on** a minor league team.
8. His batting average **is** 363.
9. **Yeah**, Billy! We wish you luck!

CHAPTER 1

The Noun

Almost everything and everyone in the world has a name. We need to name things and people so that we can talk about them.

- A *noun* is a word that names a person, place, thing, or idea.

Before you begin the lessons in this chapter, do the Warm-Up exercise. It will help you find out how well you understand this part of speech.

Warm-Up.   Find the nouns in these sentences. List them in order on your paper.

1. Last year Alex got a part-time job.
2. He saved his money and bought a used car.
3. His state requires owners to buy insurance.
4. He had to make several decisions.
5. The cost was high, but Alex got full coverage.

Lesson 1. Finding Nouns in Sentences

A noun is a word that names a person, place, thing, or idea. Examples:

Person: The insurance **agent** sold Alex a policy.

Place: Most **states** require car owners to have insurance.

Thing: Alex saved his **money** and bought a **car**.
            The **door** was squeaky, but Alex fixed it.

Idea: Alex had to make a **decision**.
            The athlete had much **courage**.

Activity A.   Name ten nouns that belong in each group listed below. Two examples are given in parentheses. Write the lists on your paper.

1. time (day, second)
2. places (garage, city)
3. things (book, coat)
4. amounts (size, liter)
5. events (concert, party)
6. persons (student, man)
7. actions (race, trip)
8. qualities (honesty, trust)

Nouns can be categorized in three ways: common or proper, abstract or concrete, and collective. Each category will be discussed separately.

A *common noun* is the name of a general type of person, place, thing, or idea.

A *proper noun* is the name of a particular person, place, thing, or idea.

A common noun is capitalized only if it is the first word of a sentence or part of a title. A proper noun is always capitalized.
Examples:

Common Nouns	Proper Nouns
president	George Washington
athlete	Babe Ruth
race horse	Bold Venture
book	*Robinson Crusoe*
author	Pearl S. Buck
place	Alaska
day	Tuesday
document	the Constitution
movie	*Gone With the Wind*

Activity B. Write this list of common nouns on your paper. Write a proper noun beside each common noun. Write a common noun beside each proper noun.
Examples:

    actress — Elizabeth Taylor
    Canada — country

1. teacher
2. city
3. country
4. dog
5. actor
6. planet
7. president
8. newspaper
9. neighbor
10. singer
11. street
12. band
13. movie
14. holiday
15. Bugs Bunny
16. the World Series
17. Harvard
18. French
19. Atlantic Ocean
20. Ohio
21. Thanksgiving

22. river	25. month	28. Reggie Jackson
23. baseball player	26. high school	29. Star Wars
24. football team	27. television show	30. Ireland

Activity C.   Write this list of words. Capitalize only the words that are proper nouns. A proper noun names a *particular* person, place, thing, or idea.

1. school	11. benji
2. actor	12. road
3. florida	13. america
4. ocean	14. paper
5. michael j. fox	15. john wayne
6. china	16. christmas
7. lake	17. mr. wilson
8. july	18. carpenter
9. mars	19. california
10. england	20. wednesday

Activity D.   Write the following sentences. Capitalize the proper nouns.

1. Last summer we drove to utah and saw the great salt lake.
2. A ruby is the birthstone for people born in july.
3. The author of *the sea wolf* was jack london.
4. The capital of austria is vienna.
5. In his last game, babe ruth hit three consecutive home runs.

- The name of a particular place is a proper noun. The name of a country, state, city, street, or building is a proper noun.
  Examples:

Common Nouns	Proper Nouns
city	New York City, Los Angeles
river	the Mississippi River
street	Main Street
apartment	Apartment 103
route	Route 96
high school	Montgomery High School
park	Rock Creek Park

- An abbreviation is a short form of a word. If the whole word is a proper noun, you capitalize the abbreviation.
  Examples:

Proper Noun	Abbreviation
Maryland	MD
Doctor Smith	Dr. Smith
Main Street	Main St.

- Parts of the country are proper nouns. Directions are common nouns.
  Examples:

Part of the country: I visited the **South** last spring.
Direction: I am going **south** next spring.

Activity E. Write each of the following sentences. Capitalize the proper nouns. Every sentence will have at least one proper noun.

1. Robert mailed a package to houston, texas.
2. His friend lives at 602 river drive, apartment 119.
3. Last year robert went to a new high school.
4. He liked northview senior high very much.
5. Robert and sue went swimming in the lake.
6. The lake was at the end of north shore drive.

Activity F. Most of the words in an address are proper nouns. Write each of these addresses on your paper. Capitalize all of the proper nouns. Abbreviate when possible.

1. mr. joe keller
   route 2, box 206
   marshall, iowa 50152

2. mrs. karen thompson
   99 norris avenue
   waterloo, new york 13165

3. mr. c. j. simmons
   1580 eaton way
   burke, virginia 22015

4. miss pam williams
   41 maple lane
   lyon, california 94104

Activity G. Write these sentences on your paper. Capitalize the proper nouns. Not every sentence will have a proper noun.

1. When alex graduated from high school, he took a trip to the south.
2. On the first day, he drove 300 miles southwest.
3. He started in baltimore and spent the first night in north carolina.
4. On the second day, alex drove west to visit some friends in tennessee.
5. The next day alex headed southeast to florida.

- The name of a language and a particular course are proper nouns. The name of a subject is a common noun.
  Examples:

Proper Nouns	Common Nouns
English, French	language
History I	social studies
Algebra	math

- A title is a proper noun. Books, songs, movies, and people are some of the things that can have a title. The first word and all main words in a title are capitalized.
  Examples:

Reverend Frank Garcia	*Lord of the Rings*
"The Star Spangled Banner"	*The Red Pony*

Activity H.   Read each sentence below. Write the sentences as they should appear.

1. Karl got an A in (English, english).
2. Next year Alex is taking (math and social studies, Math and Social Studies).
3. Jennifer signed up for (math I, Math I).
4. Cara enjoys (physical education, Physical Education).
5. Danny is going on a field trip in (earth science II, Earth Science II).

Activity I. Write each of these sentences on your own paper. Capitalize all of the proper nouns.

1. On wednesday alex came home from florida.
2. His sister jennifer was watching television.
3. "Hello, alex," jennifer said. "Welcome home from the south."
4. "Your boss, mr. jackson, called you yesterday," Jennifer told him.
5. "He wants you to report to the office on millstream drive tomorrow."
6. "Thanks," alex said. "Why are you home? I thought you were taking a french class."
7. "The class meets in the morning. How about taking me for a ride in your new car? I'd like to go south myself."
8. "OK," alex agreed. "Let's go."

* A *collective noun* is the name of a group of people, places, or things.

Groups of people: group, audience, crowd
Groups of places: United States, Europe
Groups of things: herd, flock, collection

* The name of people or things may be written as two or more words. Sometimes the words are written separately. Sometimes, hyphens are used.
  Examples:

White House   son-in-law   ice cream
Dr. Ed Tyler   Maple Street   Secretary of State

Activity J.   Read the sentences below. Find five nouns that name a group of things or people. List the words on your paper.

1. The baseball team practiced every day.
2. Alex's club had a meeting every Thursday.
3. The whole neighborhood went to the picnic.
4. Carla decided to join the navy.
5. The jury found the man innocent.

Activity K.   Find all of the nouns in these sentences. Make a list of them on your paper.

1. A forget-me-not is a lovely blue flower.
2. The vice-president spoke at our graduation.
3. Mount McKinley National Park is in Alaska.
4. Jane was the maid-of-honor at the wedding.
5. Kim took her toothbrush and toothpaste on the trip.

•   A noun may be abstract or concrete.

       A *concrete noun* is a word that names something you can see or touch.

       An *abstract noun* is a word that names something you can think about or talk about. You cannot see it or touch it. An abstract noun is an idea.

Concrete Nouns	Abstract Nouns
money	cost
clock	time
school	education
steel	strength

Activity L.   Read each pair of words. On your own paper, write the abstract noun in each pair.

1. fever   thermometer
2. law   judge
3. price   price tag
4. pizza   hunger
5. year   calendar
6. earthquake   disaster

Lesson Review

Lesson Review.   Make a list of all of the nouns in these sentences. State whether each noun is common, proper, concrete, abstract, or collective.

1. Alex Jones wanted very much to buy a car.
2. Every week he saved a certain amount of money.
3. He put his money in a bank and received interest.
5. He wanted a small car that would get good gas mileage.
6. Alex saw an ad in the newspaper.
7. He called the phone number and made an appointment.
9. Then he found the perfect car. The price was right.
10. Alex had a good feeling. He made the purchase.

Lesson 2. Singular and Plural Nouns

A *singular noun* is the name of *one* person, place, thing, or idea.

A *plural noun* is the name of *more than one* person, place, thing, or idea.

- Most plural nouns end in *-s* or *-es*. When the plural noun ends in *-es*, the plural has an extra syllable. You can hear the difference if you say the words aloud.
  Examples:

Singular Nouns	Plural Nouns
ship	ships
group	groups
path	paths
church	churches
dish	dishes
six	sixes

Activity A. Make each of these singular nouns plural. Add either an *-s* or *-es*. Say the plural aloud. You will hear the extra syllable when the plural noun ends in *-es*.
Examples:

town — towns   guess — guesses

1. bunch*es*
2. address*es*
3. car
4. fox ✓
5. book
6. school
7. ladder
8. mountain
9. ax ✓
10. watch ✓
11. wish ✓
12. witch ✓
13. idea
14. tax ✓
15. sled
16. patch ✓
17. bench ✓
18. river
19. quiz ✓
20. icicle

Activity B.   Number your paper from 1-20. Next to each number, write whether the word is singular or plural.

1. action	6. reports	11. feet	16. summer
2. bunches	7. forest	12. doctor	17. bosses
3. team	8. majority	13. Alex	18. men
4. Main Street	9. agents	14. nations	19. towns
5. circus	10. address	15. committee	20. crowds

- Nouns that end in -*y* and have a consonant before the -*y*, become plural by changing the -*y* to -*i* and adding -*es*.

- Nouns that end in -*y* and have a vowel before the -*y*, become plural by simply adding an -*s*.

Nouns That Change		**Nouns That Do Not Change**	
city	cities	key	keys
lady	ladies	alley	alleys
spy	spies	boy	boys

Activity C.   Write the list of nouns below. Make each noun plural. Examples:

turkey — turkeys   county — counties

1. monkey	6. injury
2. chimney	7. army
3. country	8. navy
4. body	9. bay
5. journey	10. day

Activity D. Find the spelling mistakes in these sentences. Write the sentences correctly.

1. The spys from the two countrys were both ladys.
2. Thier bodys were completely covered with soot after they cleaned the chimneys.
3. Those boys fell and received many injurys.

- The plural of most nouns that end in *-f* or *-fe* is made by adding *-s*.
  roof, roof**s**   chief, chief**s**

- Some nouns that end in *-f* or *-fe* change the *-f* to *-v* and add *-s* or *-es*.
  leaf, lea**ves**   calf, cal**ves**   knife, kni**ves**

- The plural of some nouns ending with a consonant and an *-o* is formed by adding *-es*. Others add only the *-s*.
  hero, hero**es**   photo, photo**s**
  tomato, tomato**es**   hairdo, hairdo**s**

- The plural of nouns ending with a vowel and an *-o* is formed by adding *-s*.
  radio, radio**s**   rodeo, rodeo**s**

- A few nouns become plural by changing letters within the word.
  man, m**e**n   foot, f**ee**t   mouse, m**i**ce
  woman, wom**e**n   tooth, t**ee**th   goose, g**ee**se

- Some singular and plural nouns are spelled the same.
  deer   sheep
  trout   series

Activity E.   Find the spelling mistakes in these sentences. Write the sentences correctly.

1. Last winter the mans shot two deers.
2. The rancher bought eighty sheeps.
3. We went fishing and caught seven trouts.
4. The Reds won two World Serieses in a row.
5. They ate six loafs of bread and ten potatos.

Activity F.   Write the plural of each of these singular nouns. Then, use the plural in a sentence.
Example:

    goose-geese.   The **geese** honked as they flew.

1.	calf	11.	tomato
2.	belief	12.	potato
3.	foot	13.	mouse
4.	man	14.	hero
5.	tooth	15.	deer
6.	foreman	16.	chief
7.	team	17.	bus
8.	knife	18.	moose
9.	lady	19.	chairman
10.	monkey	20.	elf

Lesson Review

Part A.   Read the following paragraph. Find six plural nouns. List them in order on your paper.

The traffic in front of the house was heavy for about two hours. About twenty people came to the party. Everyone seemed to be wearing new clothes. The guests stood in small groups around the snacks and around the stereo. They talked about their summer fun and the year to come.

Part B.   Write the plural of each of these nouns.

1.	woman	13.	dish
2.	sheep	14.	potato
3.	goose	15.	address
4.	tomato	16.	deer
5.	life	17.	path
6.	hero	18.	agent
7.	key	19.	party
8.	spy	20.	knife
9.	child	21.	trout
10.	city	22.	mouse
11.	tax	23.	stereo
12.	policy	24.	business

Lesson 3. Nouns That Are Possessive

A noun that is possessive shows ownership or a relationship. A possessive noun has an apostrophe.

Examples:

Ownership: That car belongs to Alex.
                 That is **Alex's** car.

Relationship: Jennifer is the sister of Alex.
                 Jennifer is **Alex's** sister.

Remember that most plural nouns end in -*s* or -*es*. A noun that is possessive also ends in -*s*. Plurals and possessive nouns sound the same when they are said aloud. Many people get plurals and possessives mixed up when they write them. A written possessive noun looks different from a plural noun because the possessive noun uses an apostrophe. Look at the examples below. Notice the difference in the meaning.

Plural Noun	**Possessive Noun**
We bought two **records**.	The **record's** cover is lost.
I read three interesting **books**.	The **book's** author autographed it.
The **planes** had engine trouble.	The **plane's** propellor was broken.

Activity A.   Decide if the boldfaced word in each sentence is a plural or a possessive. Write the word. Then write the word plural or possessive after it.
Example:

Chicago has some of the **world's** tallest buildings.
world's — possessive

1. **Alex's** insurance policy came in the mail.
2. The policy had several **pages**.
3. A few of Alex's **friends** stopped by the house.
4. They came to see their **friend's** new car.
5. They went out to inspect the **car's** tires.
6. The **tires** were brand new.

A possessive noun can be singular or plural. Study the examples below.

* Make a singular noun possessive by adding -'s.

Singular	**Singular Possessive**
teacher	teacher**'s** desk
child	child**'s** bike

* Make a plural noun that ends in -s possessive by adding only an apostrophe.

Plural	**Plural Possessive**
teachers	teachers' meeting
trees	trees' leaves

- When a plural noun does not end in *-s*, make it possessive by adding *-'s*.

Plural	Plural Possessive
men	men**'s** department
children	children**'s** room

Activity B. Write the possessive nouns in each sentence. Write singular or plural after each word.

Example:

The **ladies'** department had a sale. **ladies'**—plural

1. The albums' covers were all lost.
2. The cat slept on the sofa's cushion.
3. Alex had to replace the television's picture tube.
4. The mice's tracks led under the baseboard.
5. Last week the children's room was painted.

Activity C. Write the singular and plural possessive form for each word.

Examples:

club   club's clubs'
lady   lady's ladies'

1. chapter	6. president	11. job	16. audience
2. agent	7. child	12. thing	17. man
3. person	8. church	13. noun	18. foot
4. state	9. crowd	14. goose	19. sunflower
5. fox	10. navy	15. wife	20. monkey

- A number of common expressions contain possessive forms. Many refer to time or to price.
  Examples:
  ten dollars' worth
  one day's trip
  three days' vacation

Activity D. Write the correct word that should appear in each sentence.

1. Mark likes to put in his two (cents', cent's) worth.
2. Alex gets two (weeks, week's) vacation every year.
3. You will only have a (minutes', minute's) wait.
4. I'd like five (dollar's, dollars') worth of stamps.
5. We hoped for a rest at the (week's, weeks) end.

Lesson Review

Part A. Write the possessive nouns in these sentences. Add apostrophes where they are needed.

1. Alexs job is very important to him.
2. He has worked in Mr. Wilsons store for one year.
3. Mr. Wilson sells mens sports clothes.
4. Every week at the salespersons meeting they talk about their work.
5. Mr. Wilsons plan is to make Alex a manager some day.

Part B.   Write the boldfaced noun in the sentences below. Identify each one as a plural noun or a possessive noun. Add an apostrophe if it is needed.
Example:

Several **years** ago, Terri and Jake went to New York.
   years — plural noun   (no apostrophe is needed)

1. Terri and Jake went to New York City with their **parents**.
2. They wanted to see the **worlds** tallest buildings.
3. **Jakes** favorite place was the Statue of Liberty.
4. One of the **familys** most enjoyable places was Lincoln Center.
5. Terri and her mother shopped for **womens** clothes.
6. Jake and his father went to Madison Square Garden to see a few boxing **matches**.
7. The **crowds** of people and the subways were exciting.
8. At the **trips** end, they all hoped to go again soon.

CHAPTER REVIEW

Part A.   Write the nouns in each sentence. Be sure to include possessive nouns.

1. The party was over.
2. Jake and Terri let their parents go into the room.
3. Mrs. Griffin looked at the living room.
4. Records, glasses, and empty bowls were everywhere.
5. Jake and Terri cleaned up their friends' dirty dishes.
6. It was the end of a great evening.

Part B.   Find and capitalize all of the proper nouns in the following sentences.

1. The summer was almost over. In august terri and Jake would both return to school.
2. Terri was going to be a senior at wilson high school.
3. Jake was going to hanover community college.
4. He also planned to work part-time at mr. jackson's store.
5. Terri was taking french, math, and science.
6. Jake was taking english and business subjects.
7. Jake remembered his trip to the south.
8. When his english teacher asked him to write a composition, he had a good topic.
9. He decided to title his paper "my first trip to florida."

Part C.   Write the plural form of each of these singular nouns.

1. wolf
2. city
3. quiz
4. teacher
5. student
6. monkey
7. house
8. party
9. child
10. tooth

Part D.   Write the word that should appear in each sentence to make it correct.

1. Jake and his friend (brian, Brian) went to the movies.
2. They were seeing (*star wars*, *Star Wars*) for the fifth time.
3. The theater had special prices on (wednesday, Wednesday).
4. They were going to the (Early Show, early show).
5. Jake had to study for an (english, English) test.
6. Brian also went to (hanover community college, Hanover Community College).
7. Brian was taking (Basic Computers I, basic computers I).
8. He planned to become a (computer operator, Computer Operator).
9. On the way home there was a lot of (traffic, traffics).
10. Jake and Brian talked about their (colleges, college's) team.
11. They wondered about the (teams' , team's) chances.
12. When they got home, (Jakes, Jake's) sister was waiting.
13. Brian had been one of (Terri's, Terris) heroes for years.
14. "Did you get your (dollar's, dollars) worth?" Terri asked.
15. "Yes. It is the (worlds, world's) best show!" he said.

CHAPTER 2

The Pronoun

When we speak or write, we identify the person or thing we are talking about. The word we use to name the person or thing is a noun. After we have said or written the name, we may use another part of speech to refer to the person or thing. The part of speech that we use is a *pronoun*.

- A pronoun is a word used in place of a noun.
- The noun that the pronoun replaces is called the antecedent.

John is a senior.   **He** is on the track team.
Pronoun—**He**   Antecedent—**John**

Katie is a student.   **She** is a cheerleader.
Pronoun—**She**   Antecedent—**Katie**

Before you begin the lessons, do the Warm-Up exercises. You will find out how well you understand pronouns.

Warm-Up A. Find six pronouns in these sentences. List them in order on your paper.

1. Katie looked for her new homeroom.
2. She walked up the stairs to the third floor.
3. Katie found an old friend. They were in the same homeroom.
4. "This must be the place," said Katie.
5. "Lucky us!" laughed Laura.
6. "At least we won't be late the first day!"

Warm-Up B. The pronoun in each of the following sentences is in boldface. List each pronoun on your paper. Then, write the noun that the pronoun has replaced.

1. Laura and Katie are both seniors. **They** are old friends.
2. Ms. Delente is the homeroom teacher. **She** also teaches French.
3. James Melcher is in the class. Katie has known **him** for years.
4. "Can I have your phone number?" James asked Katie. "Here **it** is," Katie said.
5. "Please call **me** this evening," Katie said.

Warm-Up C. Write these sentences. Choose the correct pronoun from each pair given in parentheses.
Example:

Laura and Katie found <u>their</u> homeroom. (their, her)

1. Laura and _____ are in the same French class. (I, me)
2. Please walk _____ girls to class. (we, us)
3. _____ room is yours? (Which, What)
4. Everyone is trying to find _____ first period class. (his, their)
5. James went to his class by _____ . (hisself, himself)

Lesson 1. Personal Pronouns

A pronoun is a word that replaces a noun. Without pronouns, we would have to repeat the same nouns over and over again. Examples:

Susan said that Susan was going to call Susan's mother.
Susan said that **she** was going to call **her** mother.

Remember that every pronoun has an antecedent. This antecedent is the noun that the pronoun refers to. The pronoun must agree with the antecedent in person, case, number, and gender.

Katie is going to call her mother.
She is leaving now.
Katie is the antecedent for the pronoun *she*.

There are several kinds of pronouns. The first kind that you will study is the personal pronoun.

- *Personal pronouns* distinguish between the speaker, the person spoken to, and the person or thing spoken about.
  Examples:

The first person is the speaker.
  I am late.

The second person is the person spoken to.
  You are late.

The third person is the person spoken about.
  He is late.

- Personal pronouns express number. They can be singular or plural.
  Examples:

  Singular (one)   **Plural (more than one)**
  I am late   **We** are late.
  She is leaving.   **They** are leaving.

- Personal pronouns express gender. The three genders are *masculine* (male), *feminine* (female), and *neuter* (those that are neither masculine nor feminine).
  Examples:

  Masculine   **Feminine**   **Neuter**
  He is tall.   **She** is my friend.   **It** is a notebook.

- Personal pronouns express case. The case reflects the way the pronoun is used in a sentence.

  The three cases are *nominative* (the pronoun is used as the subject), *objective* (the pronoun is used as the object), and *possessive* (the pronoun shows ownership).
  Examples:

  Nominative: **He** is in my French class.
  Objective: I know **him**.
  Possessive: That book is **his**.

Personal Pronouns

	Nominative	Objective	Possessive
Singular			
First person	I	me	my, mine
Second person	you	you	your, yours
Third person	he, she	him, her	his, her, hers
	it	it	its
Plural			
First person	we	us	our, ours
Second person	you	you	your, yours
Third person	they	them	their, theirs

Activity A.   Use the chart above to help you with this activity.
Examples:

first person, singular, nominative:	**I**
second person, plural, possessive:	**your, yours**
third person, singular, objective, masculine:	**him**

1. third person, plural, nominative
2. third person, singular, objective, neuter
3. first person, plural, possessive
4. second person, singular, objective
5. third person, plural, possessive
6. first person, singular, objective
7. second person, singular, possessive
8. second person, plural, nominative

Activity B. Which pronoun could be used to replace each boldfaced word or groups of words? Write your answers on your own paper.
Example:

I saw **Mary** yesterday. — I saw **her** yesterday.

1. I have **a hammer and a saw**.
2. **The gloves** are lost.
3. **An airplane** is flying overhead.
4. I wrote a letter to **George**.
5. **Sara's** house is in the country.
6. "That book is **Katie's**," Katie said.
7. "That is **Laura and Katie's** room," Katie said
8. "**Katie** is late," Laura said.
9. **Carol and** I are going to the dance.

Activity C. On your own paper, rewrite each of the sentences below. Use a pronoun to replace the words that are in boldface.
Example:

At the end of the first day of school, **Gina** was tired.
At the end of the first day of school, **she** was tired.

1. **Gina and Karen** waited for the school bus.
2. "The teacher gave **Gina** homework," Gina said.
3. Gina decided to do **her homework** as soon as she got home.
4. **Gina's** homework was not difficult.
5. The teacher told **Gina** to write a paragraph in French.
6. "What is the paragraph about?" **Karen** asked.
7. "What I did on **Gina's** vacation, of course!" Gina laughed.

Activity D.   Make a list of all the personal pronouns in these sentences. Then, next to each pronoun, write its antecedent.
Example:

Finally **Corey and Beth** got on **their** bus.
Corey and Beth is the antecedent for the pronoun *their*.

1. Jennifer had her French book.
2. She and Michelle talked all the way home.
3. They laughed about a joke they had heard.
4. "I am hungry," Jennifer said.
5. "You can stop by my house," Michelle said.   "We can fix a hamburger."
6. "A hamburger sounds very good to me," Jennifer said.

- *-self* pronouns are used in two cases.
        I hurt **myself**.
        This indicates an action done to yourself.

        He ate the whole pie **himself**.
        This shows emphasis.

Self Pronouns

	Singular	Plural
First person	myself	ourselves
Second person	yourself	yourselves
Third person	himself, herself, itself	themselves

Lesson Review

Lesson Review. Read these sentences and find the personal pronouns. List them on your own paper. Write the antecedent beside each one.

1. The first day of school was over. It had been very pleasant.
2. Katie enjoyed her new classes.
3. She went to the movies by herself.
4. She also enjoyed seeing her old friends.
5. Katie went to her room to do her French homework by herself.
6. She wondered if James Melcher would call.
7. She hoped that he would.

Lesson 2. Relative Pronouns

The relative pronouns are *who*, *whom*, *whose*, *which*, *that*, and *what*. Like personal pronouns, all relative pronouns must agree with their antecedents.

Who, *whom*, and *whose* refer to people.
Which and *what* refer to things.
That refers to people or things.

The compound relative pronouns are *whoever*, *whomever*, *whichever*, and *whatever*. The antecedents of compound relative pronouns are not stated. The antecedents refer to a group of persons or things that are known to the listener or reader.
Examples:

Whoever wants to go swimming should come now.
You may choose **whichever** shoes you want.

Activity A.   Write these sentences on your paper. Then, circle the relative pronouns.

1. The car that Gary bought is blue and white.
2. Gary wanted a car that had four doors.
3. Gary's friend, who is a mechanic, inspected the car.
4. Gary prefers cars that have four doors.
5. Gary also had a friend whose father owned a garage.

Activity B.   Read these sentences.   The relative pronouns are in boldface. List them on your paper. Write the antecedent beside each one.
Example:

> The car **that** Gary bought is blue and white.
> > *that* refers to *car*

1. The man **who** owned the garage sold Gary new tires.
2. There is the man **whom** I met last week.
3. Andy likes cars **that** have four-wheel drive.
4. The mechanic has a car **that** is an antique.
5. Did you see the screwdriver **that** I was using?

Activity C.   Read these sentences.   Make a list of all of the relative pronouns on your own paper.

1. Do whatever you think should be done.
2. My sister, who wants to be an actress, tried out for the school play.
3. My dog, which is a miniature schnauzer, barks at everyone.
4. You may have whatever you want for dinner.
5. Here are the shoes that I bought.
6. Andy had a friend whose cousin caught a forty-pound fish.
7. Whoever wants to go first should come upstairs now.
8. I found what I wanted.

Activity D.   Read the list of words below. Find all of the pronouns and write them on your paper.

1. himself	8. bus	15. friend
2. whoever	9. lady	16. you
3. car	10. Ms. Wise	17. whatever
4. Andy	11. I	18. themselves
5. which	12 what	19. its
6. that	13. whom	20. happiness
7. he	14. school	21. she

Activity E.   Read the list of pronouns below. Make two lists on your paper. Name one list personal pronouns. Name the other list relative pronouns. Write each word under the appropriate column.

1. we	8. you	15. whom
2. that	9. who	16. whichever
3. which	10. ours	17. that
4. what	11. them	18. themselves
5. mine	12. whose	19. whoever
6. its	13. us	20. whatever
7. I	14. itself	21. he

Activity F.   Read each sentence. Choose the correct pronoun from the words in parentheses. Write the complete sentence.

1. There are the shoes _____ I want. (who, that)
2. My dog, _____ is a St. Bernard, eats anything. (who, which)
3. There is the lady _____ I met last week. (whom, what)
4. I like a house _____ has a big yard. (who, that)

Lesson Review

Lesson Review.   Read these sentences. Make a list of all the relative pronouns.   Include the compound relative pronouns.   Write the antecedent beside the pronoun.
Example:

> I like food **that** is very spicy.
>   *that* refers to *food*

1. The mechanic who checked Gary's car did a good job.
2. Gary said to Andy and Frank, "Whoever wants to go for a ride should come now."
3. You may choose whichever shoes you want.
4. There is the man that I met in Florida.
5. We have steak and chicken. You may have whichever you prefer.
6. Gary had a friend whose sister was in the play.
7. Did you see the hat that I was wearing?
8. Mrs. Jones has a coat that is genuine mink.
9. I got what I wanted for my birthday.
10. Shamus, who is my cat, scratched me on the face.

Lesson 3. Pronouns That Ask Questions

An interrogative pronoun introduces a question. These pronouns are *who*, *which*, and *what*.
Examples:

Who is planning the dance?
Which shoes did Katie buy?
What page is the homework assignment on?

Interrogative pronouns may also be used as relative pronouns. *Who*, *which*, and *what* are interrogative pronouns only when they ask a question.
Examples:

Interrogative: **Who** is going with Andy to the dance?

Relative: Andy asked a girl **who** is in his class.

Activity A.   Read these sentences carefully.   Make a list of the interrogative pronouns on your paper.

1. Which season of the year do you like best?
2. What is the name of your book?
3. Tell me who is going to the dance.
4. Do you know what the answer is?
5. Who is your favorite singer?

• Interrogative pronouns must agree with their antecedents. In these cases, the antecedents are actually the answers to the questions that are asked.
Examples:

Who refers to a person or persons.
   Who is your English teacher?
   Who are the teams in the Super Bowl this year?

What refers to things, places, or ideas.
   What is the name of your street?
   What is your answer?

Which can refer to people or things. Use *which* when the answer is a choice between two or more definite things.
   Which team will win the game?
   Which newspaper do you read?

Activity B.   Write these sentences on your paper. Choose the correct pronoun from the pair given in the parentheses.

1. ___ of these fish is larger? (Which, What)
2. ___ do you want for dinner? (Which, What)
3. ___ will win the World Series? (Who, What)
4. ___ is the name of your school? (Which, What)
5. Kevin wondered ___ to ask to the dance. (whom, which)
6. ___ plays third base for the team? (Who, Which)
7. ___ is the world's tallest building? (Who, What)

Activity C.   Read these sentences carefully. Find five relative and five interrogative pronouns. Make two lists on your paper and put the appropriate pronouns under each column.
Example:

Which shoes are the ones **that** you like best?

Interrogative Pronouns	Relative Pronouns
which	that

1. Gary has a friend whose uncle lives in Canada.
2. Name all of the states that you have visited.
3. What is the name of your book?
4. Choose whichever book that you want.
5. Tell me which book you like best.
6. Who is the coach of your baseball team?
7. Which tree is taller?
8. What is your favorite subject in school?
9. Do whatever you think is best.

Lesson Review

Lesson Review.   These sentences contain pronouns (personal, relative, and interrogative).   Find these pronouns and list them in order on your own paper.   Name the kind of pronoun that each one is.
Example:

Who is the man **that I** saw yesterday?

> **Who** — interrogative
> **that** — relative
> **I** — personal

1. It was Friday night. Gary and Andy wondered what they would do.
2. "What is playing at the movies?" Gary asked.
3. "Whatever is there is okay with me," Andy said.
4. "Whom should we ask to go with us?" Gary said.
5. "I think that I will ask Katie," Andy answered.
6. Gary thought for a moment about which girl he could ask.
7. "What is the name of Katie's friend?   Is it Laura? I think that I will ask her," Gary decided.
8. Do whatever you think is best.

Lesson 4. Demonstrative Pronouns

Demonstrative pronouns point out persons and things. The demonstrative pronouns are *this*, *these*, *that*, and *those*.

Singular: **This** book is mine.
Plural: **These** books are mine.

Singular: **That** house is expensive.
Plural: **Those** houses are expensive.

This and *these* point out persons and things that are close. *That* and *those* point out persons and things that are farther away.

This is my house.   **That** is my house.

Activity A.   Write these sentences on your paper. Circle all of the demonstrative pronouns.

1. Did Laura enjoy that movie?
2. Those socks are new.
3. Put these clothes in the hamper.
4. Hang that coat up, please.
5. This is my neighbor, Mrs. Loomis.
6. Those flowers are beautiful.
7. These are my favorite pictures.

Activity B. Read the following sentences. Choose the correct pronoun in parentheses. Write the whole sentence on your paper.

1. Did you see ____ shooting star? (this, that)
2. ____ is my house. (This, These)
3. Look across the street. ___ are new houses. (These, Those)
4. ____ people just moved in. (That, Those)
5. Mrs. Jones handed Katie a package. "You may open ____ now," she said. (this, that)

Lesson Review

Lesson Review. You have become familiar with four kinds of pronouns. They are personal, relative, interrogative, and demonstrative. Find the pronouns in the sentences below. List them in order. Name the kind of pronoun that each one is.
Example:

Who was the lady **that I** saw yesterday?
    Who — interrogative
    that — demonstrative
    that — relative
    I — personal

1. Gary works at a store which sells men's clothes.
2. "Which evenings am I working this week?" he asked.
3. "Whichever nights that you want," said his boss, Mr. Jackson.
4. Gary decided on the hours that he wanted.
5. "What department am I in tonight?" Gary asked.
6. "Go to the stockroom and help them with inventory."
7. Gary asked those who were working what he could do first.
8. He helped the people whose job was counting shoes.

Lesson 5. Indefinite Pronouns

Indefinite pronouns replace nouns that are understood by the listener or reader. These nouns may not have been mentioned in the sentence. Some indefinite pronouns are always singular. For example, *everyone* is singular because it refers to every single person. Examples:

Correct: Everyone **is** going to the beach.
Incorrect: Everyone **are** going to the beach.

The following is a list of singular indefinite pronouns:

one	some	someone
something	somebody	anyone
anything	anybody	everyone
everything	everybody	no one
nothing	nobody	none
much	another	all
each	one another	each other
any	every	either
neither	many a	

* Other indefinite pronouns are always plural.

several	others	both
few	many	

Examples:
Several have arrived.   The **others** will be here soon.

- Some indefinite pronouns may be singular or plural. You must read the sentence carefully and understand its meaning. In the examples below, the verbs show whether the pronouns are singular or plural.

    Singular: **"All** <u>is</u> well," the town crier said.
                Some of the house <u>has</u> been remodeled.

    Plural: **All** of the boys <u>are</u> going to the concert.
                Some of the houses <u>have</u> been remodeled.

- The indefinite pronoun may be used as the antecedent for another pronoun.
    Examples:

    All of the boys ate <u>their</u> lunches.
    All is plural and is the antecedent for *their*.

    Every **one** of the girls has <u>her</u> ticket.
    One is singular and is the antecedent for *her*.

- If the gender of the indefinite pronoun is not clear, you may use the masculine pronoun. You may also use both the masculine and feminine pronouns.
    Examples:

    Each person brought <u>his</u> notebook.
    Everyone brought <u>his</u> or <u>her</u> ticket.

Activity A. Read these sentences. Make a list of the indefinite pronouns on your paper.

1. Everyone brought food to the picnic.
2. Jack did not know anyone at the party.
3. None of the boys was late.
4. Try to be nice to one another.
5. Few of the students liked liver.
6. Everyone talked to the bride at the wedding.
7. Every one of the people brought a present.
8. Sam saw no one that he knew.
9. Cathy knew some of the people in the class.
10. Everything is ready for the party.
11. Try to help each other.
12. Some of the food was too spicy.
13. Karl knew nothing about the Red River.
14. Sally knows someone in that neighborhood.
15. Other than Sara, I do not know a person in that school.

Activity B. Write these sentences. Use the correct word in the parentheses.

1. Everybody ___ coming to the party. (is, are)
2. Everything in the closet ___ Katie's. (is, are)
3. Some of those people ___ going home now. (is, are)
4. Someone ___ reading that book. (is, are)
5. Somebody ____ my pencil. (has, have)
6. Everyone must leave ___ coat on. (his, their)
7. Each girl brought ____ own paper. (her, their)
8. All of the men brought ___ wives. (his, their)
9. None of the children remembered ____ lunch. (his, their)
10. Every one of those coats is missing ___ buttons. (its, their)

Activity C. Use each of these indefinite pronouns correctly in a sentence.

1. someone
2. everyone
3. no one
4. anybody
5. nothing
6. none
7. everything
8. something
9. all
10. nobody

Lesson Review

Lesson Review. Find ten indefinite pronouns in these sentences. List them in order on your paper.

1. Everyone in Mr. Jackson's store was decorating for fall.
2. All of the employees came to work that day.
3. Everybody was quiet as he or she worked.
4. Nobody said anything.
5. Suddenly someone laughed.
6. "Why are we all so quiet?" someone said.
7. "No one has anything to say!" said Mr. Jackson.

CHAPTER REVIEW

Pronouns replace nouns in sentences. You learned that a pronoun must agree with its antecedent. The antecedent is the word or words that the pronoun is replacing in a sentence.

Before you do the exercise below, review the five kinds of personal pronouns.

Pronoun	Examples
Personal pronouns	*I, you, he, she, it , they, theirs*
Relative pronouns	*who, which, that, whatever*
Interrogative pronouns	*which, who, what*
Demonstrative pronouns	*this, that, these, those*
Indefinite pronouns	*anyone, all, nobody, everything*

Part A.   The pronouns in these sentences are in boldface. List the pronouns on you paper. Beside each pronoun, write the kind of pronoun it is.

Example:

That is the **one that I** like best.

That — demonstrative	**that**— relative
one — indefinite	**I** — personal

1. **It** was the dry season of the year.
2. **Everyone** was watering **his** yard.
3. **No one** was expecting rain for a week.
4. "**Everybody** must take **his** or **her** turn," Mr. Jones announced.

THE PRONOUN

5. **"Who** wants to water tonight?"
6. **"That** isn't a hard job," Katie said.
7. **She** went outside and watered **everything** thoroughly.
8. **"I** will take **my** turn tomorrow night," Gary said.
9. **They** did **what** had to be done until the rain came.

Part B. Write each sentence. Choose the correct word given in parentheses.

1. Gary decided to build (hisself, himself) a stereo.
2. (Which, What) kind should I buy?
3. (Which, Who) of my friends will help me?
4. Gary chose the friend (which, that) knew the most.
5. Nobody (are, is) as smart about electronics as Andy.
6. Gary handed Andy the directions. "You can read (these, those)," he said.
7. I think we can do this (ourself, ourselves).
8. (Us, We) guys won't have any problem at all.
9. "I think this kit is missing some of (its, it's) parts."
10. "Do (whatever, whichever) needs to be done," Gary said.
11. Soon they had put the parts together (theirselves, themselves).
12. They looked at the finished stereo. The music (this, that) will play will be terrific!

CHAPTER 3

The Adjective

An *adjective* is a word that describes a noun or pronoun. Adjectives may be used to limit or to change the meaning of a noun or pronoun.

- Most adjectives come before the noun that they are describing.
    The **sleepy** child was crying.

- *Predicate adjectives* come after the noun or pronoun that they are describing.
    He is **tired** and **hungry**.

- Adjectives are sometimes placed after the noun for emphasis. Then, they are set off from the rest of the sentence with commas.
    The tree, **wet** and **shimmering**, swayed in the breeze.

Warm-Up A. Find the adjectives in these sentences. List them on your paper in order.

1. The autumn day was cool and clear.
2. Everyone was happy about the beautiful weather.
3. After school, Sharon and Diana went for a long walk.
4. They admired nature, wondrous and splendid.

Warm-Up B. List the boldfaced adjectives on your paper. Next to each adjective, write the noun or pronoun being described. Example:

The **new** car was **expensive**.
    new — car
    expensive — car

1. The students in **Sharon's** homeroom had a meeting.
2. They elected **new** officers for the **school** year.
3. "Sharon is **smart**, **loyal**, and **fun**," said Diana.
4. "She will be a **good** president."
5. The election was **close**, but Sharon won.

Warm-Up C. List the boldfaced words in these sentences on your paper. Identify the part of speech of each word. It may be a noun, a pronoun, or an adjective.

1. That **history** book belongs to James Melcher.
2. James takes **history** during the second period.
3. They all went to the **meeting** room.
4. The **meeting** began at three o'clock.
5. The **south** wind was warm.
6. The wind came from the **south**.

Lesson 1. What is an Adjective?

An adjective is a word that describes a noun or pronoun. It can name a characteristic of someone or something.

The **sleepy** child is crying.
She is **sleepy**.
That is a **wonderful** idea.
David was **late** for work.
David sells **men's** clothes.

- An adjective can limit the noun by giving a number or quantity.

    There are **three** trees.
    Several people arrived late.
    They lived in the house for **many** years.

- Demonstrative adjectives are used to point out someone or something.
    Did you see **that** boy?
    Those people are in **my** class.

- Possessive adjectives are used to show ownership.
    Diana went to **her** class.
    David and Vince saw **their** favorite movie.
    Vince's house is on the corner.

Activity A.   List the adjectives in these sentences.

1. David has a part-time job at Mr. Jackson's store.
2. The store sells sporting goods and men's clothes.
3. David works in many different departments.
4. His favorite department is fishing equipment.
5. "Those new reels are expensive," David thought.
6. "I will save my money and buy one."

- Adjectives help make your meaning clear. They can make a sentence more interesting, too.

    Jake was ready for dinner.
    Tall, **mean** Jake was ready for **a big** dinner.

- Several adjectives can be used to tell more things about a person or object in a sentence.

    I live in **that large white colonial** house.

        Which one? **that** one
        How big?   **large**
        What color? **white**
        What kind? **colonial**

Activity B.   Read these sentences. All of the adjectives are in boldface. List them on your paper. Beside each adjective, write the noun or pronoun that is described.

Examples: She is **tall**.   The **old empty** house is for sale.

           tall — she   **old** — house

                                  empty — house

1. David bought an **expensive new** reel.
2. He planned a **fishing** trip with **his** friends.
3. "**This** reel will be **great**," he said.
4. "I am **sure** that I will catch **several big** fish."
5. David and Vince left early the **next** morning.
6. They were very **hopeful**.

Activity C.   Read these sentences. Find the adjectives. List them on your own paper. Beside each adjective, write the noun or pronoun that it describes.

1. The lake was beautiful on that morning.
2. David saw a large fish jump in the water.
3. Vince used his trusty old rod and reel.
4. They fished for eight hours.
5. By late afternoon they had caught many fish.
6. They were tired but happy with themselves.

Activity D.   Rewrite these sentences on your paper. Add one or more adjectives before each boldface noun.

1. Students brought **books** to **class**.
2. **People** brought **food**.
3. **School** started early.
4. I saw **mountains** and **rivers**.
5. Diana planted **tomatoes** and **cucumbers**.

Activity E.   Add as many adjectives as you can to these sentences. Write the new sentences on your own paper. Circle all of the adjectives in your sentences.

1. Diana has a dog.
2. David bought a coat for his sister.
3. The fisherman cast his line into the lake.
4. It was morning.
5. The store had a sale.
6. I have a job.
7. Ray plays piano.
8. My jacket has a hole in it.

Lesson Review

Lesson Review.   Find the adjectives in these sentences.   Make a list of the adjectives on your paper. Beside each one, write the noun or pronoun that the adjective describes in the sentence.

1. In October the weather can be chilly.
2. David decided to wear his winter coat.
3. He had several classes on Wednesdays.
4. David's favorite class was math.
5. Math was easy for him.
6. He drove to the college in his car.

Lesson 2. The Articles — A, An, The

The articles, *a*, *an*, and *the*, are adjectives. They are placed before nouns in sentences.

- The articles *a*, *an*, and *the* are always used as adjectives. The definite article is *the*. Use *the* when you are talking about a particular person or thing. The indefinite articles are *a* and *an*. Use *a* or *an* when you are talking about a general group of people or things.

    I saw **the** movie yesterday.

    Sharon ate **an** apple for lunch.

    Vince caught **a** fish.

    Give me **the** book.

        In this example, the person wants a certain book.

    Give me **a** book.

        In this example, any book will do.

- Use the article *a* before a word that begins with a consonant sound. Use the article *an* before a word that begins with a vowel sound.

    a large apple   **a** tough assignment

    an apple   **an** assignment

- The article *a* is used with singular nouns. The article *the* can be used with singular and plural nouns.

    I bought **a** car.   *Car* is singular.

    David bought **the** car.   *Car* is singular.

    He bought **the** books.   *Books* is plural.

Activity A.   Write these sentences on your paper. Circle all of the articles.

1. The math class was the first class of the day.
2. The students had a homework assignment.
3. The first part of the class was easy.
4. The class discussed the answers to the problems.
5. "I got a different answer to the problem," David said.
6. The teacher explained the problem.
7. She used an overhead projector.
8. Later she made a new assignment.

Activity B.   Write these sentences on your paper. Use the correct article in the parentheses after each.

1. Diana packed ___ apple for her lunch. (a, an)
2. They waited for ___ hour. (a, an)
3. The teacher made ___ long assignment. (a, an)
4. They had ___ English lesson. (a, an)
5. The children fed ___ elephant at the zoo. (a, an)
6. We built ___ igloo in our backyard. (a, an)
7. Look up the topic in ___ index. (a, an)
8. The principal posted ___ honor roll. (a, an)
9. Not ___ one of them was late. (a, an)
10. Jack is ___ honest man. (a, an)

Activity C.   Write these sentences on your paper. Choose the correct article in the parentheses for each.

1. Look at ___ coat with the fur collar. (a, the)
2. Did you enjoy eating ___ peaches? (a, the)
3. Mrs. Jones put ___ groceries on the table. (a, the)
4. We went to New York City to see ___ play. (an, the)
5. Chicago is ___ American city. (a, an)
6. They did ___ activity in class. (a, the)

Lesson Review

Lesson Review.   Number your paper from 1 to 10. Write the correct article for each sentence.

1. A hammer is ___ useful tool. (a, an)
2. Did you see ___ pencils I left here? (a, the)
3. Where is ___ envelope? (a, an)
4. I was in ___ earthquake in California. (a, an)
5. We have ___ eight-foot tree in our yard. (a, an)
6. Have you ever seen ___ bald eagle? (a, an)
7. At the zoo we looked at ___ snakes. (a, the)
8. They did ___ math activity. (a, an)
9. "What ___ ugly dog," she said. (a, an)
10. What happened to ___ flower vase? (a, the)

Lesson 3. Adjectives That Are Capitalized

Proper adjectives are made from proper nouns. They are capitalized.

Proper noun:	He is an **American**.
Proper adjective:	He is an **American** soldier.
Proper noun:	I went to visit **France**.
Proper adjective:	I enjoyed the **French** food.

Activity A.   Read these sentences. Make a list of the proper adjectives on your own paper. Not all of the capitalized words will be proper adjectives, so read very carefully.

1. Sharon had French first period.
2. She almost forgot her French book.
3. In her English class, Sharon was studying Shakespearean literature.
4. She liked American literature better.
5. Mr. Thomas was teaching them about Indians in social studies.
6. He brought in some Indian blankets and jewelry to show the class.
7. Then Sharon went to her career education class. It was a Wednesday-only class.

Activity B.   Use these proper adjectives in sentences. Be sure that you use them as adjectives that describe nouns or pronouns.

1. Spanish
2. German
3. Chinese
4. Democratic
5. French
6. Swiss
7. American
8. Olympic

Activity C.   Write these sentences on your paper.   Add a proper adjective in each space.

1. We ordered _____ dressing.
2. Mr. Jones likes _____ cheese.
3. Diana studied the _____ language last year.
4. Those people are _____ citizens.
5. He belongs to the _____ political party.
6. The class studied _____ tribes of Mexico.
7. Harry Winston is a _____ artist.
8. He just bought a _____ truck.

Activity D.   Number your paper from 1 to 10. Decide if the boldfaced word is a noun or an adjective.   Write your answer beside each number.

1. I like **French** designers.
2. Mark lives in **Philadelphia**.
3. He is a **Philadelphia** boy.
4. **Frank** is as normal as blueberry pie.
5. He wrote an **Irish** derby on St. Patrick's Day.
6. I am late for my **French** lesson.
7. Next summer I want to visit **Spain**.
8. I'd like to study **Spanish** first.
9. Where is my **Spanish** book?
10. The book is in the **Chevrolet** truck.

Lesson Review

Lesson Review.   Write these sentences on your paper. Capitalize all of the proper adjectives.

1. Diana has a german sheperd named Hiedi.
2. Hiedi likes to ride in the ford truck.
3. Hiedi also likes swiss cheese.
4. The rest of the family prefers american cheese.
5. That dog thinks that she is a swiss dog.
6. Hiedi is actually quite famous. A spanish artist painted her.

Lesson 4. Numbers Used As Adjectives

Numbers can be used as adjectives. The number describes the noun by telling how many.
Examples:

Mrs. Jones canned **twenty** jars of pears.
Seventeen people came to the party.

The indefinite pronoun can also be used as an adjective when it is used to describe a noun or a pronoun. The indefinite pronoun suggests a number. However, the exact amount is not given.
Examples:

Several years went by before I saw her.
They lived in that house **many** years.
All students must report to class.

Activity A.   Here is a list of ten words that can be used as adjectives. Use each one in a sentence. Be sure you are using the word as an adjective that describes a noun or pronoun.

1.	few	6.	much
2.	eighty	7.	most
3.	one	8.	thirty-three
4.	some	9.	several
5.	three	10.	all

Activity B. Read these sentences. The boldfaced words are adjectives. List them on your paper. Write the noun that each word describes beside it.
Example:

> **Many** people read that book.
> **Many** — people

1. **Twenty-five** people signed up for the class.
2. **One** student dropped out.
3. After a **few** weeks, the teacher gave a test.
4. **Several** members of the class got 100 percent.
5. **Most** students enjoyed the class.

Activity C. Read these sentences. All of the words that show quantity or number are in boldface. List them on your paper. Identify which part of speech each one is.
Example:

> **All** of the students signed up for **six** classes.
> **All** — pronoun
> **six** — adjective

1. The hurricane winds were **eighty** miles an hour.
2. The storm lasted for **several** hours.
3. **Everyone** on the block watched the storm.
4. **Many** trees blew down in the neighborhood.
5. We watched as a **few** cars drove through the storm.
6. **Most** people stayed inside.
7. The electricity was out for **six** hours.
8. **No one** could cook dinner or watch television.
9. **Some** families went out for dinner.
10. **Others** tried to barbecue in their yards.

Lesson Review

Lesson Review. List the adjectives in these sentences. Beside each, write the noun it describes.

1. On Sunday, several friends visited City Zoo.
2. They fed peanuts to three chimpanzees.
3. Sara counted eight lions and six tigers.
4. There were many monkeys.
5. William ate three hot dogs and drank some lemonade.
6. "All birds seem to like to sing," Chris said.
7. "I would like to stay here several hours."
8. Few people wanted to go home.

Lesson 5. Possessives and Demonstratives Used As Adjectives

Some nouns or pronouns in the possessive case can be used as adjectives. In a sentence these words are used to describe. The possessive noun or pronoun tells us something about the noun it is describing.

Possessive nouns used as adjectives:
Diana's dog is a German sheperd.
We went to the **world's** fair.
There is **Mr. Jackson's** store.

Possessive pronouns used as adjectives:
My house is on the corner.
That wagon has lost **its** wheels.
Whose room is that?

• A possessive noun can be used with a possessive adjective.

That is **my sister's** book.

The possessive noun *sister's* describes book.
Whose book? *Sister's* book

The possessive adjective *my* describes sister's.
Whose sister? *My* sister

Activity A. In these sentences, the possessives used as adjectives are in boldface. Make a list of them on your paper. Beside each one, write the noun that the word is describing.

Example: **His** cap was left in **Mr. Jackson's** store.

                His — cap

                Mr. Jackson's — store

1. I always like to get **my money's** worth.
2. Naturally, I shop in **Mr. Jackson's** store.
3. **His** store is close to **my** house.
4. In the **men's** department, there were some wool sweaters.
5. I bought one for **my father's** birthday.
6. **His** birthday will be next Saturday.
7. I still remember **our** fun buying last **year's** presents.
8. **Dad's** face lit up when he opened them.

Activity B. Find the possessives used as adjectives. List them on your paper. Then, write the noun each possessive adjective is describing.

1. Jack's bike is missing.
2. His coat was in the living room.
3. My mother's ring was lost.
4. There was a rabbit in my garden.
5. Whose pencil is this?

The demonstrative pronouns — *this, that, these,* and *those* — can be used as adjectives. They answer the question, *which one?*

     Pronoun: **That** is a mistake.
     Adjective: **That** mistake was Vince's.

Activity C.   The demonstratives in these sentences are in boldface. Decide which ones are used as adjectives and which ones are used as pronouns.

1. "**This** Sunday let's go together and watch the football game," Leslie said.
2. "Do you think **that** team will win a game **this** year?" David asked.
3. "Some of **those** new players are better," Leslie answered.
4. " I especially like **that** new fullback from Penn State."
5. "**This** should be a good season," David said.
6. "**That** remains to be seen," said Leslie.

Activity D.   Write these sentences.   Circle five demonstrative adjectives. Then draw an arrow to the noun each describes.
Example:

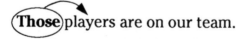

(Those) players are on our team.

1. The football game that day was exciting.
2. "Where are those snacks you promised?"
3. "Look in that cupboard over the refrigerator."
4. "That is where my mother keeps those things."
5. "These potato chips look good. Now, where are the sodas?"

Lesson Review

Lesson Review.   Find the possessives used as adjectives in these sentences. List them on your own paper in order. Beside each one, write the noun that the adjective is describing.

1. David and Vince did their homework together.
2. Vince's answer to problem 7 was wrong.
3. "Explain your answer to me," Vince said.
4. David tried to explain his answer.
5. There was a frown on Vince's face.
6. "Maybe my answer is wrong, too," David said.
7. "Let's both check our work," Vince suggested.
8. Vince's suggestion was helpful.
9. "Now, let's get some of your mother's great dessert," Vince said.
10. Together they raided David's refrigerator.

Lesson 6. Using Adjectives to Make Comparisons

Many adjectives are used to compare people or things. There are three degrees of comparison: *positive*, *comparative*, and *superlative*.

Positive	Comparative	Superlative
strong	stronger	strongest
easy	easier	easiest
big	bigger	biggest
careful	more careful	most careful
popular	less popular	least popular
good	better	best
bad	worse	worst

- Use the positive to describe one thing.
- Use the comparative degree to compare two things.
- Use the superlative degree to compare more than two things.
    - Correct: Sam is **younger** than Roger.
    - Incorrect: David is Sharon's brother. He is the **oldest**.

- Most one-syllable adjectives form their comparative and superlative degrees by adding *-er* and *-est*.

Activity A. List these adjectives on your paper. Write the comparative and superlative degrees beside each one.
Example: **tall** — taller, tallest

1 young
2 old
3 kind
4 short
5 green

6. slow
7. late
8. strict
9. bright
10. nice

• Some two-syllable adjectives form their comparative and superlative degrees by adding *-er* and *-est.* Others form their comparative and superlative degrees by using *more* and *most* or *less* and *least.*

Positive	Comparative	Superlative
careful	more careful	most careful
happy	happier	happiest

• Compare adjectives of more than two syllables by using *more* and *most* or *less* and *least.*

Positive	Comparative	Superlative
wonderful	more wonderful	most wonderful
successful	more successful	most successful
excited	less excited	least excited
generous	less generous	least generous

• Some adjectives form their comparative and superlative degrees in an irregular way.

Positive	Comparative	Superlative
good	better	best
bad	worse	worst

Activity B.   Read these sentences. The adjectives are in boldface. List them on your paper. Beside each one, identify the degree of comparison.
Examples:

> Danny is the **most helpful** person I know.
> That blanket is **soft**.
> She is **stronger** than her sister.
> > **most helpful**—superlative
> > **soft**—positive
> > **stronger**—comparative

1. That is the **least comfortable** chair.
2. Chris thought the movie was **terrible**.
3. The girl was the **most talented** actress in the play.
4. I have never seen a **sadder** face.
5. This coat is **less expensive** than the other one.

Activity C.   Use each of the following adjectives correctly in a sentence.

1. least useful
2. smaller
3. most successful
4. more wonderful
5. less careful
6. better
7. worst
8. heaviest
9. lighter
10. best

Activity D.   Write each sentence. Use the correct word from the pair given in parentheses.

1. That is the (reddest, most red) sunset I have ever seen.
2. Which of those two buildings is (taller, tallest)?
3. Sharon hopes to be (thinner, more thin) in two weeks.
4. St. Augustine is the (oldest, older) city in Florida.
5. This chair is the (more, most) comfortable of the two.
6. That movie was the (goodest, best) I have seen.
7. Yesterday's homework was (easier, easiest) than today's.
8. Roger is the (least, less) generous person I know.
9. Karen is (successfuller, more successful) than Mac.

Lesson Review

Lesson Review. List the ten boldfaced adjectives. Identify the degree of comparison of each adjective.

1. David is **older** than Sharon.
2. He is usually **nice** to Sharon, but Sharon thinks that Vince is **nicer**.
3. They both think that tennis is **fun**.
4. Sharon's forehand was **better** than her backhand.
5. "My serve is my **best** shot," David said.
6. Of the two of them, David was the **better** player.
7. Although Sharon was **strong**, David was **stronger**.
8. Sharon decided that it was **easier** to play tennis with Diana.

CHAPTER REVIEW

In Chapter 3 you found adjectives in sentences and used them correctly. Remember that a word is an adjective only if it describes a noun or pronoun in a sentence.

Read these sentences. Find all of the adjectives. List them in order on your paper. Beside each adjective, write the noun or pronoun that it describes.
Example:

The autumn day was **cool** and **clear**.
   The — day
   autumn — day
   cool — day
   clear — day

1. David and Vince decided to have a Halloween party.
2. The party was on a Saturday evening.
3. David's parents gave their permission.
4. They decorated the living room with orange and black streamers.
5. They bought the most horrible skeletons and the ugliest witches in the store.
6. Sharon found some old decorations in the attic.
7. They bought fifty red apples and ten gallons of cider.
8. Vince carved an enormous pumpkin.
9. Several people brought more food.
10. Later everyone agreed that the party was the best one yet.

CHAPTER 4

The Action Verb

An *action verb* is a word that expresses action in a sentence.

Examples:

The Wilson Wildcats **played** their first game on Saturday.
　　The verb *played* expresses action.
　　What did the Wilson Wildcats do? They *played* a game.

Melissa **looked** for Kim.
　　The verb *looked* expresses action.
　　What did Melissa do? She *looked* for Kim.

Before you begin, do the Chapter Warm-Up exercises. They will help you find out how much you already know about locating verbs and using them correctly.

Warm-Up A. Number your paper from 1 to 10. Read each sentence. Find the verb and write it on your paper.
Example:

Eric read the newspaper every morning.
read

1. The paper carrier brought the newspaper at six o'clock every day.
2. Mr. Jones heard a thud at the front door.
3. He opened the door.
4. Then he got his paper.
5. He carried it into the house.
6. Mr. Jones poured himself a cup of coffee.
7. He sat at the kitchen table.
8. First, he read the front page.
9. Next, he turned to the sports page.
10. Mr. Jones started every day the same way.

- A verb phrase contains a main verb and a helping verb.
  Examples:
  Mr. Jones **has poured** his coffee.
  main verb — **poured**   helping verb — **has**
  Now he **must go** to work.
  main verb — **go**   helping verb — **must**

Warm-Up B. Read these sentences. Find the verb phrase in each one. List the verb phrases on your own paper.

1. By six-thirty Mr. Jones has left for work.
2. Soon he is driving down Route 50.
3. All of the traffic is rushing down the highway.
4. Most of the people are going to work.
5. Everyone is thinking about the day ahead.

Lesson 1. Finding the Verb in a Sentence

An *action verb* is a word that expresses the action in a sentence. The verb tells what someone or something does, did, or will do.

Mr. Jones **read** the newspaper.
Then he **went** to work.
He **drove** his car on Route 50.
He **arrived** at seven o'clock.

- An action verb tells what the subject does.
- A sentence can have more than one verb.
- Some verbs express mental action that cannot be seen.

Mr. Jones **likes** his work.
He **thinks** about his ten o'clock meeting.

- Find the verb in a sentence by asking yourself two questions:
  1. Who or what is doing something? (subject)
  2. What are they doing? (verb)

Activity A. Read these sentences. Find the verbs. List them on your own paper.

1. Mr. Jones parked his car.
2. He greeted several of his friends.
3. They walked into the building together.
4. Mr. Jones went to his desk.
5. Then he started his work for the day.

Activity B. List the subjects and verbs in these sentences.
Example:

The secretary answered the telephone.
Subject	Verb
secretary	**answered**

1. In the office everyone worked hard.
2. Some people sorted mail.
3. Others loaded the mail on trucks.
4. The trucks hauled the mail to other places.
5. Mail carriers deliver mail.
6. The mail goes to homes and offices.
7. Mr. Jones works in an office.
8. He prepares the payroll.
9. He gives information to the computers.
10. The computer prints the checks.

Activity C. Find the verb or verbs in each sentence. List them on your own paper.
Example:

The workers went to their desks and worked.
went, worked

1. Mr. Jones parked his car and entered the building.
2. He drank some coffee and ate a doughnut.
3. He read a note from his boss.
4. His boss scheduled a meeting at ten o'clock.
5. The telephone rang.
6. Mr. Jones picked up the phone and said, "Hello."
7. He talked to the person and then hung up.
8. Then he returned to his work.

- A *verb phrase* is made up of more than one verb. A verb phrase contains a main verb and a helping verb. The helping verb *helps* the main verb to show action.
  Examples:

    Debbie **has played** soccer.
    He **had completed** the test.
    They **might have stayed** in the theater.

Activity D. Find the subject in each sentence. Then find the verb or verb phrase. List the verbs on your own paper.

1. Mr. Jones had a meeting with his boss.
2. Later he thought about the meeting.
3. The boss may have a problem.
4. Mr. Jones wondered about the solution.
5. Finally he has decided on an answer.
6. He knew the answer to the problem.

Activity E. Use each verb or verb phrase below in a sentence. Underline each subject once and each verb twice.

1. accept
2. balance
3. comfort
4. contain
5. might have examined

6. could have been
7. lift
8. pronounce
9. should remember
10. wander

Lesson Review

Lesson Review.   List the verbs in these sentences.

1. Many different people work at the post office.
2. Letters and packages stream into the post office all day and night.
3. Mail carriers collect mail from mailboxes.
4. Mail comes to the post office on trucks.
5. Airplanes also bring mail in.
6. At the post office, mail handlers unload mail.
7. Postal clerks then sort the mail.
8. People put the mail on different trucks.
9. Carriers deliver local mail the next day.
10. Every post office processes huge amounts of mail every day.

Lesson 2. Transitive and Intransitive Verbs

Two main kinds of verbs are *transitive* and *intransitive*. A *transitive verb* has an object. A verb that is transitive transfers the action from the subject to another person or thing. A sentence with a transitive verb must have a direct object. The object is a noun or pronoun. Ask a question to find the object.

John **threw** the **ball**.
John threw what? (the ball)
Ball is the direct object of the transitive verb *threw*.

Brenda **drank** the **milkshake**.
Brenda drank what? (a milkshake)
Milkshake is the direct object of the transitive verb *drank*.

James **has** a **motorcycle**.
James has what? (a motorcycle)
Motorcycle is the direct object of the transitive verb *has*.

Activity A. The transitive verb in each of these sentences is in boldface. Find the direct objects and write them on your paper.

1. Last fall Alison's band **raised** money.
2. The band members **sold** Christmas cards.
3. The band **will enter** a national contest.
4. They **want** first place.
5. Alison **will play** a trumpet solo.

- An intransitive verb does not have a direct object. The action is not transferred from the subject to another person or thing. The action expressed by an intransitive verb can be done by a person or a thing all alone. The following intransitive verbs do not have direct objects.
  Examples:

  She **is laughing**.   The fire **burned**.
  They **went** home.   The ball **bounced**.

Activity B.   Read these sentences. The verb in each sentence is in boldface. Decide whether each verb is transitive or intransitive. Write your answers on your paper.

1. Alison **is practicing** her trumpet solo.
2. She **has been practicing** for an hour.
3. She **is studying** a new song.
4. Alison **has been studying** in her room.
5. Alison **plays** very well.
6. She **plays** the trumpet very well.

Lesson Review

Lesson Review.   The verb in each sentence is in boldface. Decide whether it is transitive or intransitive.

1. Bruce **drove** Brenda to her home.
2. They **talked** about the concert.
3. Brenda **could read** Bruce's lips.
4. She also **used** sign language.
5. They **enjoyed** the evening.

Lesson 3. Verbs Also Express Tense

The verb in a sentence also expresses tense, or time. Verbs use endings, helping verbs, or both to express tense.

The first part of the verb is the present tense. The infinitive form of the verb is *to* plus the present tense. The second part of the verb is the past tense. The past tense of regular verbs is formed by adding *-ed* to the infinitive. To express future tense, use the helping verb *will* or *shall* with the first part of the verb. The present, past, and future tenses are called the simple tenses.

Infinitive: **to fish**
Present Tense: I **fish** in that lake.
                 (to show an action done in the present time)
Past Tense: I **fished** in that lake.
                 (to show an action done in the past)
Future Tense: I **will fish** in that lake.
                 (to show an action that will be done in the future)

- Add *-s* to the present tense of the verb if the subject is singular.

Singular subject: James **practices** every day.
Plural subject: The players **practice** every day.

Remember: collective nouns (names of groups acting as one) are singular. Indefinite pronouns, such as *everyone*, are also singular.

Singular subject: The team **practices** after school.
Plural subject: Both teams **practice** after school.
Singular subject: Everyone **wants** a victory.

Activity A.   Read each of these sentences. The verb is in boldface. Identify the tense of the verb in each sentence. Write your answers on your own paper.

1.   The Wilson Wildcats **will play** their first football game on Saturday.
2.   The team **practices** every day.
3.   They **wondered** about their opponents.
4.   The coach **called** the team together.
5.   He **talked** to them about the game plan.
6.   "I **believe** in you guys."
7.   The team **knows** the plan.
8.   They **want** a victory on Saturday.

Activity B.   Choose the correct verb form (singular or plural) to use in each sentence below. Write it on your own paper.

1.   James _____ for a victory. (hope, hopes)
2.   He _____ tackle on the team. (play, plays)
3.   He _____ to practice every day. (go, goes)
4.   Greg and Lorenzo both _____ quarterback. (play, plays)
5.   The coach _____ which one will start. (decide, decides)
6.   Everyone _____ forward to the games. (look, looks)
7.   The whole team _____ hard. (work, works)

The Perfect Tenses

The three perfect tenses are: present perfect, past perfect, and future perfect.

Present Perfect: James **has tackled** his opponent many times.
- Use this tense to show an action started in the past and continuing up to the present. The idea is that this action is likely to be done again.

Past Perfect: James **had tackled** him before the whistle blew.
- Use this tense to show one action completed before another past action.

Future Perfect: In a few minutes, our team **will have won** the game.
- Use this tense to show an action that will be completed before a certain time in the future.

The perfect tenses are also called the compound tenses. The perfect tenses are formed by combining different tenses of the helping verb *have* with the third part of the verb. Most verbs in the English language are regular. The third part of a regular verb is formed by adding *-ed* and is called the past participle. However, *have* is an irregular verb. You must learn the different forms of *have* so that you can write the perfect tenses correctly.

(To) Have

Present Tense (sing.)   James **has** the football now.
                      (plural)   They **have** nine points.
Past Tense   The team **had** the lead.
Future Tense   The team **will have** a victory. (or **shall have**)
Present Perfect (sing.) He **has had** the ball three times.
                      (plural) They **have had** the ball most of the game.
Past Perfect   When the quarter ended, they **had had** enough.
Future Perfect   In one week, we **will have had** a winning season.

- The verb *have* can be a main verb or a helping verb.
  Have as a main verb: I **have** a good team.
                                   (*have* used alone)
  Have as a helping verb: I **have** scored a touchdown.
                                   (*have* used with another verb)

Activity C. Write these sentences on your own paper. Choose the correct form of the verb *have* for each sentence.

1. The Wilson Wildcats _____ the football. (has, have)
2. The team _____ scored a touchdown. (has, have)
3. The Wildcats have _____ the ball for most of the quarter. (have, had)
4. The other team will _____ had few chances. (has, have)
5. We soon will _____ the victory. (have, had)

Activity D. Decide whether *have* is the main verb or the helping verb in each sentence. Write your answers on your own paper.

1. The quarterback has had a good day.
2. He has thrown several good passes.
3. Howard has a good record so far.
4. He has one win and no losses.
5. He has high hopes for the future.

Activity E.   Write the present perfect, past perfect, and future perfect tenses in sentences for each verb below.
Example:

jump— He **has jumped**. He **had jumped**. He **will have jumped**.

1. act	6. offer
2. discuss	7. open
3. improve	8. pass
4. lock	9. snarl
5. move	10. whisper

Activity F.   Write all six tenses of each verb below, using the third person singular (he, she or it).
Example:

whisper

present:	She **whispers**.
past:	She **whispered**.
future:	She **will whisper**. (or **shall whisper**)
present perfect:	She **has whispered**.
past perfect:	She **had whispered**.
future perfect:	She **will have whispered**.

1. walk
2. work
3. fish
4. drive
5. roar

• Remember: Most verbs in the English language are regular. They form their past and perfect tenses by adding *-ed* to their present form.

- When a verb ends in -y and the letter before the -y is a consonant, change the -y to -i and then add the ending for the tense.

> I **worry** every day.
> She never **worries**.
> He **worried** all day.

Activity G.   Use a form of the verb in the parentheses to complete each sentence. List the verbs in the correct tense for each sentence. Spell them correctly on your paper.

1. Yesterday Kim _____ tennis. (play)
2. Andy _____ for a job last week. (apply)
3. Melissa _____ a new dress once a month. (buy)
4. Last year James _____ on the football team. (play)
5. Eric _____ last week's football game. (enjoy)
6. This morning they _____ to school. (hurry)
7. Sandra _____ to Aunt Emily's letter. (reply)
8. Yesterday he _____ home from school. (stay)
9. A loud thunderstorm _____ me. (terrify)
10. The witness _____ for two days during the trial. (testify)

- The past participle is the third part of the verb. It is used with *have*, *has*, or *had* to form the perfect tenses of irregular verbs. Look at these commonly used irregular verbs.

Present	Past	Past Participle
begin	began	(have) begun
catch	caught	(have) caught
choose	chose	(have) chosen
come	came	(have) come
eat	ate	(have) eaten
give	gave	(have) given
go	went	(have) gone
know	knew	(have) known
see	saw	(have) seen
teach	taught	(have) taught

Activity H. Write these sentences. Use the correct form of each verb in parentheses.

1. Ms. Lee has _____ math for many years. (teach)
2. Carol _____ her old bike to her sister. (give)
3. Howard _____ an old friend at the movies. (see)
4. They have already _____ their dinner. (eat)
5. Have you ever _____ that movie? (see)
6. Phillip had _____ his homework already. (begin)
7. Jackie _____ the answer to the question. (know)
8. The fielder _____ the deep fly ball. (catch)
9. The news _____ on TV at six o'clock. (come)
10. Where has Monica _____ ? (go)
11. Saturday everyone _____ to the game. (go)
12. I finally have _____ my new coat. (choose)

- The words in a verb phrase may be written together. However, they may be separated by another word in the sentence.

    Has Donna **gone** to the store?
    She **has** finally **written** the letter.
    Michael **will** probably **do** his work.

Activity I.   List the verb phrases in these sentences on your own paper. Ignore any words that come between the helping verb and the main verb.

1. James has always given his best.
2. That bell has never rung on time.
3. Have you heard that record before?
4. Victor has often seen him before.
5. I have not seen him before.
6. Have you ever studied French?
7. Carl will probably bring his lunch.
8. Jane and Sam have never gone to a museum.
9. She had always had good luck.
10. Barbara had seldom enjoyed a book so much.

Activity J.   Write the tense of each verb or verb phrase given in boldface.

1. **Will** you **drive** me to the store?
2. Yesterday Beth **lost** her gloves.
3. Ms. Potter **teaches** my math class.
4. The coach finally **chose** all of the players.
5. The Wildcats **will play** on Saturday.

6. Most of the students **came** to the game.
7. Melissa **had known** most of the players for years.
8. A reporter **has written** about many of our games.
9. His latest story **will appear** in tomorrow's paper.
10. By noon everyone in town **will have read** it.

Lesson Review

Lesson Review.   Read the story below. Find all the verbs or verb phrases. List them on your own paper. Write the tense beside each one.

Wildcats Devour Lincoln Lions

On Saturday, September 30, the Wilson Wildcat fans enjoyed a 21-3 victory over the Lincoln Lions.

Quarterback George Benetez threw two touchdown passes in the first half. The half ended at 14-0. The Lions' only score came in the third quarter with a field goal.

James Melcher made a big play late in the final quarter. He tackled the Lions' running back. He fumbled the ball. The Wildcats recovered on their 48-yard line. Wilson marched down the field and scored the final goal.

Many fans will have already extended congratulations to Melcher. We offer ours now for a fine play.

Next week the Wildcats will face the Crofton Cougars. The team hopes for a winning season. They have looked forward to the county championship for many years.

Lesson 4. The Progressive Forms

The *progressive* forms of verbs express continuing action. Compare the two sentences below.

Present: Melissa **practices** the trumpet twice a week.
                        (to show an action that is done frequently)

Present Progressive: Melissa **is practicing** the trumpet.
                        (to show an action being done now)

A progressive form is a verb phrase. It is made from a form of the verb *be* + the present participle.

The fourth part of the verb has the ending *-ing* and is called the present participle. Notice the examples of the progressive tenses made from the verb *work* and the subject *he*. The present participle of *work* is *working*.

Examples:

Present progressive: He **is working**.
Past progressive: He **was working**.
Future progressive: He **will be working**.
Present perfect progressive: He **has been working**.
Past perfect progressive: He **had been working**.
Future perfect progressive: He **will have been working**.

Activity A.   Read the sentences.   Find the verb in each one.   Write it on your own paper.

1. The band is practicing now.
2. Cathy was practicing her flute when the phone rang.
3. Soon Tom will be practicing the drums.
4. Sam has been practicing for thirty minutes.
5. Melissa had been practicing the trumpet when I interrupted her.
6. In five minutes, the band will have been practicing for an hour.

- Learn the different forms of the verb *be* so that you can write the progressive tenses correctly.   Notice the difference in the singular and plural forms.

(To) Be

Simple Tenses

Present	Past	Future
I am	I was	I will be
you are	you were	you will be
he is	he was	he will be
we are	we were	we will be
you are	you were	you will be
they are	they were	they will be

Perfect Tenses

Present Perfect	Past Perfect	Future Perfect
I have been	I had been	I will have been
you have been	you had been	you will have been
he had been	he had been	he will have been
we have been	we had been	we will have been
you have been	you had been	you will have been
they have been	they had been	they will have been

Activity B. Write these sentences. Use the correct form of the verb *be* in each space.

1. I have _____ on an airplane six times.
2. Jack will _____ going to Seattle next week.
3. Doris has _____ in my class every year.
4. By noon today Mac will have _____ working for four hours.
5. Sara _____ leaving for Florida on Friday.

Activity C. Write a correct sentence for each of the verbs below.

1. will have been going
2. has been working
3. had been eating
4. is beginning
5. was writing
6. were whispering
7. am opening
8. am moving

Activity D. Write the tenses of each boldfaced verb phrase.

1. Mario **had** never **gone** to Texas before this year.
2. He **is flying** there for a vacation.
3. He **will be leaving** at noon.
4. Mario **has been packing** all morning.
5. His father **called** for him.
6. They **are going** to the airport now.

Activity E.   In each of these sentences, the main verb is missing. Write the sentence on your paper. Use the correct word from the pair given in parentheses. Examples:

- Use the present participle (verb + -*ing*) with any forms of the helping verb *be*.

    Sheila **is fixing** her bike.

- Use the past participle form (verb + -*ed*) with any forms of the helping verb *have*.

    Sheila **has fixed** her bike.

- If the verb phrase includes both *have* and *be*, use the present participle. (verb + -*ing*)

    Sheila **has been fixing** her bike.

1. Melissa has been _____ the trumpet for several years. (playing, played)
2. She has _____ in the Wilson band for two years. (playing, played)
3. This year the band is _____ to Florida for a national contest. (going, gone)
4. Some of the parents will be _____ the band. (accompanying, accompanied)
5. The band members have been _____ money all year. (raising, raised)
6. So far they have _____ more than one thousand dollars. (raising, raised)
7. In the fall everyone is _____ Christmas cards. (selling, sold)
8. So far, they have _____ a thousand boxes. (selling, sold)
9. Melissa herself has _____ two boxes this week. (buying, bought)
10. She will be _____ cards soon after Thanksgiving. (addressing, addressed)

Lesson Review

Part A. Write a sentence using the verb *sharpen* in each of the six regular tenses and the six progressive forms. *Sharpen* is a regular verb. The first one has been done for you.

1. present — Phillip **sharpens** his pencil before class.
2. past
3. future
4. present perfect
5. past perfect
6. future perfect
7. present progressive
8. past progressive
9. future progressive
10. present perfect progressive
11. past perfect progressive
12. future perfect progressive

Part B. Now, read the paragraph below. List the verb or verb phrase in each sentence. Write the tense beside each one.

Louis Armstrong played the trumpet. He earned a special place in American history. As a child he lived in an orphanage in New Orleans. There he first studied the cornet. In 1922, he played on a Mississippi riverboat. He joined a band in Chicago. Then in 1924, Armstrong moved to New York City. Soon he was playing the trumpet. He invented a completely new style. By 1925, he was recording his music. Later he formed his own band. People also loved his husky voice. In the 1930's, Armstrong starred in movies. His popularity continued for the rest of his life. One of his records, "Hello, Dolly!" sold two million copies in 1964. Armstrong died in 1971. People will remember this man and his music for a long time.

Lesson 5. The Emphatic Form — The Verb With *Do* or *Did*

The helping verbs *do* and *did* are used to emphasize the negative word, such as *not*.

> Many stores **do** *not* **close** on holidays. (present)
> Dan **did** *not* **find** his book. (past)

The helping verbs *do* and *did* are also used to form questions.

> **Do** you **like** strawberries? (present)
> **Did** you **finish** that book? (past)

The helping verbs *do* and *did* are used only with the present form of the main verb.

> **Did** you **go** home? (The verb *go* is present.)

The emphatic form is used only to express present and past time.

> I **do** *not* **want** to be late for lunch. (present)
> Frank **did** *not* **find** his coat. (past)

• The verb *to do* can also be used as a main verb. The main verb *do* means "to perform an action." It can be used in all tenses.

Present:	Brigette **does** her chores early.
Past:	Victor **did** his work well.
Future:	Everyone **will do** his part.
Present perfect:	The family **has done** its work well.
Past perfect:	We **had done** the yard work by dinner time.
Future perfect:	Soon he **will have done** his lessons.

Activity A.   Find all the verbs and their helpers in these sentences. List them on your own paper.

1. Did you see Cathy at lunchtime?
2. Jack never did find his gloves.
3. The family is doing the dishes.
4. Do you read the newspaper?
5. Where do you do your homework?

Activity B.   Decide whether *do* is a helping verb or a main verb in each sentence below.
Example:

> Soon he **will have done** his report.
> **will have done** — main verb

1. After dinner Eric and Melissa **did** the dishes.
2. Finally they **had done** their chores.
3. Melissa **had** already **done** her homework.
4. "**Did** you **see** my math book?" Eric asked.
5. "You **are** always **doing** something with that book!" Melissa laughed.
6. "I **did** not **see** it today," he said.
7. At last Eric **did find** the book.
8. Soon he **was doing** his math.

Lesson Review

Lesson Review.   Write the verb and any helper for each sentence. Then, identify the tense.

1. In the fall, people do extra yard work.
2. Did you rake your leaves yet?
3. They have already raked their yard.
4. Does your family plant grass seed in the fall?
5. Soon they will have done the whole yard.
6. I have already done my part.
7. Did Dad do the front yard yet?
8. The boys are doing their part.
9. They did not trim the trees this year.
10. Did you find all of the verbs?

Lesson 6. The Conditional Forms

Some helping verbs put a condition on an action. A condition is a requirement or a responsibility.

May — Might	He **may** succeed. He **might** succeed.
Can — Could	He **can** sing. He **could** sing.
Shall — Should	You **shall** leave. You **should** leave.
Will — Would	The basket **will** hold a bushel. He **would** like that movie.
Must	I **must** go now. You **must** find your paper. They **must** leave quickly.

Now, look carefully at the main verbs in the verb phrases above. They are all present tense verbs.

- The conditional helping verbs are irregular. Do NOT add an -s to the verb when you use it with a singular subject.

Singular Subject	Plural Subject
He **may** go. Jack **must** leave.	They **may** go. The men **must** leave.

- All of the other regular verbs and irregular verbs DO either add an -*s* or change to a different form.

Singular Subject	Plural Subject
He **sings** well.	They **sing** well.
He **has gone**.	They **have gone**.
She **is going**.	They **are going**.

- The conditional form may be combined with the compound tenses.

Present Perfect Tense:	I **have gone**
Conditional Form:	I **could have gone**
	He **might have gone**
Present Progressive Form:	I **am going**
Conditional Progressive:	I **could be going**
	They **must be going**

- In some sentences, the main verb is not included. It is understood. Example:

Are you doing your homework?

No, but I should.

(The rest of the verb phrase *do my homework* is understood.)

Activity A. Read these sentences. Find the verb phrases. List them on your own paper.

1. You may stay there until ten o'clock.
2. Melissa can play the trumpet.
3. The basket will hold a dozen tomatoes.
4. She should do her homework.
5. She must finish her report tonight.

Activity B. Write these sentences on your paper. Add the correct word from the pair given in the parentheses.

1. Every day Andy _____ at the gym. (exercise, exercises)
2. They _____ every day. (exercise, exercises)
3. Eric _____ exercise today. (might, mights)
4. He would _____ every day if he had the time. (goes, go)

Activity C. List the verb phrase in each sentence on your own paper.

1. Melissa's purse will hold many things.
2. She should clean it up.
3. In fact, she must clean it up.
4. She cannot find anything in it.
5. Melissa should have bought a new purse.
6. She might be buying a new one.
7. Should she buy a new purse?

Lesson Review

Lesson Review. Find the verb or verb phrase in each sentence. Write each one on your own paper.

1. Next week, I might be going to Indiana.
2. I could have gone last year.
3. This year I must go.
4. I would like to leave Monday.
5. I should pack my suitcase.
6. I must take my winter coat.
7. I can go there by plane.
8. I may take only one suitcase.
9. Should I take a raincoat?
10. It might rain.

Lesson 7. Active and Passive Verbs

A verb is *active* if the subject is doing the action. The sentence tells who did what.

Carlos **wrote** a story.

A verb is *passive* if the actions happens to the subject. The sentence tells what was done by whom.

The story **was written** by Carlos.

To form the passive verb, use the helping verb *be* with the past participle (the third part of the verb).

Correct: The story **was written** by Carlos.

Incorrect: The story **was wrote** by Carlos.

- In some sentences, part of the idea is missing. The missing part is "understood." The verbs in the examples below are passive. The person who did the action is not named.

    Today the bank was robbed.   (by someone)

    The pass was thrown well.   (by someone)

Activity A.   Find the verbs in the sentences below. Decide whether each verb is active or passive. Write your answers on your own paper.

1. John Steinbeck wrote many stories.
2. *The Red Pony* was written by John Steinbeck.
3. Edgar Allen Poe wrote many poems.
4. "The Raven" was written by Poe.
5. That cake was baked by my aunt.
6. My aunt baked that cake.

Activity B. Use each verb in two sentences. First, use it as an active verb, then as a passive verb.

1. cover
2. direct
3. discover
4. disturb
5. grease
6. hit
7. invent
8. cook
9. answer
10. pack

Activity C. Read these sentences. Find the verbs and their helpers. Write them on your own paper.

1. America was discovered by Columbus.
2. We were disturbed by a loud noise.
3. The telephone was finally answered.
4. The ball was hit to left field.
5. The car was greased last month.

Lesson Review

Lesson Review. Read each sentence. Write the verb and any helper on your own paper.

1. The cotton gin was invented by Eli Whitney.
2. Cotton seeds are removed from the cotton.
3. In 1842, the Oregon Trail was explored by John Fremont.
4. Fremont was later elected as one of California's first senators.
5. *Gone with the Wind* was written by Margaret Mitchell.
6. Her book was made into a successful movie.
7. Indiana was settled in 1808 by Tecumseh, an Indian leader.
8. Tecumseh was killed at the battle of the Thames in Canada during the War of 1812.
9. In 1848, Lewis Cass was defeated by Zachary Taylor.
10. Taylor was chosen as President of the United States.

CHAPTER REVIEW

Part A. List the verbs or verb phrases that are in these sentences.

1. George Herman Ruth began playing baseball in 1914.
2. His teammates gave him the nickname "Babe."
3. He first played with the minor league Baltimore Orioles.
4. Baltimore sold his contract to the Boston Red Sox.
5. Babe pitched and batted left-handed.
6. He won many games as a pitcher.
7. In 1919, he broke all of the records for home runs in a season.
8. The New York Yankees had been looking at Ruth for some time.
9. In 1920, he was sent to the Yankees.
10. He would play in games in the outfield.
11. He continued to lead the league in home runs for many years.
12. He was hitting more home runs every year.
13. In 1927, he set a new world record.
14. He hit sixty home runs in a single year.
15. In his last game, Babe Ruth hit three home runs in a row.
16. He was elected to the Baseball Hall of Fame in 1936.

Part B. Read each sentence carefully. Choose the correct word from the pair given in the parentheses. List these words on your paper.

1. Mr. Jones _____ to work. (went, gone)
2. The Wildcats will _____ their first game on Saturday. (play, played)
3. The team _____ every day. (practice, practices)

4. They _____ a victory. (want, wants)
5. Everyone _____ to win. (like, likes)
6. He _____ never had an injury. (have, has)
7. They have _____ two touchdowns. (score, scored)
8. Monday they _____ to work. (hurryed, hurried)
9. Last week the man _____ at the trial. (testifies, testified)
10. I have _____ my work. (beginned, begun)
11. He _____ his lunch every day. (bring, brings)
12. Yvonne _____ the answer. (knowed, knew)
13. Sara always _____ her work well. (do, does)
14. The band _____ practicing now. (is, are)
15. The children _____ riding their bikes. (is, are)
16. He _____ flying to Florida. (be, is)
17. Did you _____ that book? (finish, finished)
18. Did Juan _____ home yet? (go, went)
19. He _____ go home now. (must, musts)
20. Janine _____ be finished by noon. (is, could)
21. The book was _____ by Jack London. (wrote, written)
22. That cake was _____ by Bob. (bake, baked)
23. The electric light bulb was _____ by Thomas Edison. (inventing, invented)
24. We _____ disturbed by the bell. (was, were)
25. The barking dog _____ everyone angry. (make, made)

CHAPTER 5

The State-of-Being Verb

A *state-of-being verb* tells something about the condition or state of the subject of the sentence.

- The most common state-of-being verb is *to be* and all its forms: *am, is, are, was, were, be, being, been*

  > Roberto **is** a tackle.
  >
  > He **was** on the team last year.

- Other state-of-being verbs include *appear, feel, look, taste,* and *become.*

State-of-being verbs also express tense. They may have helping verbs. The tenses of state-of-being verbs are formed in the same way as those of action verbs.

Present	Leroy **looks** happy.
Past	The water **felt** warm.
Future	She **will be** sixteen soon.
Present Perfect	He **has been** there before.
Past Progressive	They **were being** nice.
Conditional	She **could be** late.

Warm-Up A. Find the verb or verb phrase in each sentence below. Write it on your own paper.

1. My aunt is eighty years old.
2. She is looking well.
3. She always has felt healthy.
4. Aunt Marie is a good cook.
5. She has been keeping very active.

- *To be* is always a state-of-being verb when it is the main verb of the sentence. Some other state-of-being verbs can have more than one meaning. They may express a state of being or an action. If you substitute a form of *to be* for these verbs, they are linking verbs. If not, they are action verbs.

    State-of-Being Verb: The stew **tasted** good.
                                          (You could say: The stew **was** good.)
    Action Verb: Michael tasted the stew.
                                          (You could not say: Michael **was** the stew.)

Warm-Up B. Decide whether the verb in each sentence expresses action or a state of being. Write your answers on your own paper.

1. Howard finally appeared on the field.
2. He appears strong and healthy.
3. I felt the soft cloth.
4. The cloth felt soft to me.
5. She looked everywhere for her cat.
6. Her cat seemed lost.
7. The oak tree grew eight feet tall.
8. I grow radishes in my garden every year.

Lesson 1. What is a State-of-Being Verb?

A *state-of-being verb* tells something about the condition of the subject of the sentence. It does not tell what the subject is doing.

State-of-Being Verb: Roberto **is** on the football team.
Action Verb: Roberto **plays** on the football team.

In the first sentence, the verb *is* helps to make a statement about Roberto. In the second sentence, the verb *plays* tells us the action that Roberto does.

A state of being is the situation or condition of someone or something. The verb *to be* is the most common state-of-being verb. *To be* means "to exist, to live, or to happen." However, to *be* can also be a helping verb. It can be used with a main verb to express progressive tenses.

Jamie **is cooking** dinner.
She **is being** helpful.

In addition, *to be* is also used to form passive verbs. *To be* is a helping verb in those verb phrases, too.

The picture **was painted** by Norman Rockwell.
Dinner **is cooked** by Jamie on Mondays.

Here are some other commonly used state-of-being verbs:

appear	grow	seem
become	look	smell
feel	keep	stay
get	remain	taste

- State-of-being verbs also express tense.

Present	The water **feels** warm.
Past	He **looked** good yesterday.
Future	Mary **will be** fifteen next week.
Present Perfect	I **have been** hungry all day.
Past Perfect	Jack **had seemed** tired by dinner time.
Future Perfect	Carol **will have been** on a diet for a month tomorrow.

- State-of-being verbs may be used in the progressive form. Use the verb *to be* as a helping verb. Then use the present participle form (*-ing*) of the verb.

  > He **is being** nice today.
  > Carol **had been looking** good all week.
  > I **will be feeling** fine soon.

- Conditional helping verbs may be used with state-of-being verbs.

  > Karl **must be** in love.
  > I **could be** there at noon.
  > You **should look** your best tomorrow.
  > Anne **should have been** at the party.

Activity A.   Use only state-of-being verbs to make five statements about Roberto. Write your examples on your paper.
Examples:

> He **seems** nice.
> He **is** a student.
> He **grew** tall.
> He **gets** taller every year.
> He **looks** friendly.

Activity B. Find the verbs or verb phrases in the sentences below. List them on your paper. Tell whether the verb *to be* is a main verb or a helping verb in each sentence.

1. Dawn was feeling fine yesterday.
2. Today she is sick.
3. She is going to the doctor.
4. Dawn will be absent from school.
5. She will probably be fine tomorrow.
6. Dawn was given some medicine by the doctor.

Activity C. Find the verb or verb phrase in each sentence. Then identify the verb tense.

1. "The Tell-Tale Heart" is an interesting story.
2. Sam will not be here today.
3. Mrs. Frances has been in that room for two years.
4. She was a Spanish teacher.
5. I had been to New York twice.
6. We will have been there a long time.

Activity D. Write the present participle for each state-of-being verb below. Then use each verb in a sentence.
Example:

grow— **growing**   I am **growing** taller this year.

1. be   4. look
2. seem   5. feel
3. appear   6. become

Lesson Review

Lesson Review.   Each of the sentences below has a state-of-being verb as the main verb. Find the verb or verb phrase. Write each one on your own paper.

1. Ron and Jamie were ready for Thanksgiving.
2. They knew that the turkey would taste good.
3. The pumpkin pies in the oven smelled enticing.
4. Everything looked delicious.
5. "Is dinner ready yet?"
6. The whole family was hungry.
7. "I have been hungry all day!"
8. Finally, dinner was ready.
9. It is not a moment too soon for me.

Lesson 2. Action or State-of-Being?

The verb *to be* is always a state-of-being verb when it is the main verb in a sentence.

Examples:

The turkey **is** golden brown.

The turkey **is** delicious.

Many other state-of-being verbs can also be used as action verbs as well.

Examples:

Jamie **tasted** the cranberry sauce. (action verb)

The cranberry sauce **tasted** sweet. (state-of-being verb)

In the first sentence, *tasted* expresses action. Jamie did something. In the second sentence, *tasted* expresses a state of being. The condition of the cranberry sauce was sweet.

Here are examples of the different uses of several state-of-being verbs:

APPEAR

action: to come into view; to become visible

Jack **appeared** in court.

The actor **appeared** in the play.

being: to seem; to look

They **appear** friendly.

Fred **appears** taller than Mike.

FEEL

action: to touch; to think or believe
She **felt** the soft blanket.
I **feel** that you are right.

being: to be aware of a physical or mental sensation
I **feel** cold.
Denny **feels** happy.

GROW

action: to cause to grow; to cultivate
I **grew** tomatoes in my garden.

being: to come into existence; to spring up
Don **grew** two inches this year.
Orchids **grow** in Hawaii.

SMELL

action: to catch the scent or odor of something
I could **smell** the breakfast bacon.
I **smell** popcorn.

being: to have a certain scent or odor
The bread **smells** fresh.
The skunk **smells**.

Activity A. Write whether the boldfaced verb in each sentence expresses action or a state-of-being.

1. She could **smell** the smoke in the air.
2. The warm cake **smelled** inviting.
3. The oven **felt** too hot.
4. Mary **felt** the hole in her pocket.
5. Joe **grows** orange trees in Arizona.
6. She **appeared** to have a good time.
7. She has **grown** as tall as I.
8. Our cat **smells** his food before he tastes it.
9. Brad **felt** wonderful about his perfect score.
10. Nora suddenly **appeared** at the party.

If you are not sure whether a verb is a state-of-being verb, remember to try this test. Substitute a form of the verb *be* for the verb. If the meaning of the sentence is almost the same, the verb is a state-of-being verb. You cannot substitute *be* for an action verb.

| State-of-being verb: | They **remained** friends. |
| | (or) They **were** friends. |

| Action verb: | He **got** a new job. |
| | He **was** a new job. (not possible) |

Activity B. Use each verb below in two sentences. In one sentence, let the verb express action. In the other, it should express a state-of-being.

| appear | feel | grow | look |
| taste | get | keep | smell |

Activity C.   Remember that a state-of-being verb does not tell us what the subject is doing. It does not express action. Read the sentences below. Decide whether each boldfaced verb expresses action or a state-of-being. Write your answers on your own paper.

1. The Jones family **is** in the den.
2. Mrs. Jones **is reading** a book.
3. Ron **is** asleep on the sofa.
4. He **seems** tired this evening!
5. Mr. Jones **stays** awake.
6. He **is eating** an apple.
7. He **likes** a snack in the evening.
8. Jamie **appears** very busy.
9. She **must be doing** homework.
10. The television **is** on.

Activity D.   Read these sentences carefully. Find the verb or verb phrases in each one. Write it on your paper. Beside each verb or verb phrase, write the word *action* or *being*.
Examples: She **tasted** the pie.   **tasted** — action
                 Dinner **will be** ready soon. **will be** — being

1. Dinner was served at three o'clock.
2. The food looked wonderful.
3. "Dinner is looking especially good today."
4. "I want the drumstick!"
5. The sweet potatoes tasted excellent.
6. "I will have more of the corn."
7. Mrs. Jones looked pleased.
8. "I am getting full."
9. Tomorrow they will probably all be on a diet.
10. All too soon, the meal was over.

Lesson Review

Lesson Review.   List the verb or verb phrase in each sentence. Decide whether it expresses action or a state-of-being. Write your answers on your own paper.

1. Mr. Jones was looking for the newspaper.
2. He usually keeps it on the coffee table.
3. That paper gets harder to find every day.
4. Suddenly the newspaper appeared!
5. There it was on the table.
6. The newspaper appeared wrinkled.
7. It also looked torn.
8. "Who got this paper first?"
9. Mr. Jones grew angry for a moment.
10. Then he relaxed.
11. The newspaper was not damaged too much.
12. He remained in his chair with his newspaper for a while.
13. He got the news of the day.

Lesson 3. Using State-of-Being Verbs

A state-of-being verb must agree with its subject. Regular verbs and most irregular verbs add an -*s* to the present form when the subject is singular.

Singular Subject	Plural Subject
Jack **looks** happy.	They **look** happy.
Mike **feels** rested.	They **feel** rested.

The past form of the verb stays the same for singular and plural subjects.

Singular Subject	Plural Subject
Donna **looked** nice.	Both girls **looked** nice.
She **felt** wonderful.	They **felt** wonderful.

The verb *to be* is an EXTREMELY irregular verb. Whether it is a main verb or a helping verb, its form changes several times.

Singular	**Present**	**Past**
First Person	I **am**	I **was**
Second Person	you **are**	you **were**
Third Person	he **is**	he **was**
Plural		
First Person	we **are**	we **were**
Second Person	you **are**	you **were**
Third Person	they **are**	they **were**

Activity A.   Decide which form of the verb *to be* is being used in each sentence. Write your answer on your own paper.
Example:

He is Michelle's brother.
is — third person, singular, present

1. I am busy today.
2. They were happy to get the award.
3. He was depressed.
4. The band members were loud.
5. The crowd was anxious for the game to be over.
6. I was excited about my trip.
7. We were anticipating a fight.
8. It is cold in the mountains.
9. She is a careful driver.
10. They are friends of mine.

- The past participle of *to be* is *been*. Use *been* with *have*, *has*, and *had* to form the perfect tenses.
  Examples:
    Fred **has been** there before.
    They **have been** away for a week.
    Mike **had been** there for two days when he became ill.

- The present participle of *to be* is *being*. Use *being* with the helping verb *to be* to show the progressive form.
  Examples:
    Donna **is being** nice.
    Jack **was being** friendly.

- Use the verb *be* to show future tense and to show simple conditional forms.
  Examples:
  Future: He **will be** home soon.
  Conditional: Jamie **must be** late.

Activity B.   Use the correct form of the verb *to be* in these sentences. Write them on your own paper.

1. Gail _____ a cheerleader this year.
2. Megan's report _____ due yesterday.
3. They _____ all at a party last week.
4. Have you ever _____ to Yellowstone Park?
5. Yellowstone Park _____ in Wyoming.
6. The children were _____ silly.
7. "You _____ next," the nurse said.
8. I had never _____ to Columbus, Ohio, before.

Activity C.   Use the correct form of the verb *to be* in these sentences. Write them on your own paper.

1. Will you _____ at the meeting today?
2. I should _____ on time.
3. Must I always _____ the first one?
4. Can I _____ the last one?
5. Howard will _____ at practice today.

Here are some common mistakes to avoid:

1. Sometimes people are careless and leave out the *be* verb or part of the verb phrase in a sentence.

> Incorrect: The quarterback fast!
> Correct: The quarterback **is** fast!
> Incorrect: I be ready soon.
> Correct: I **will be** ready soon.

2. Sometimes people use the infinitive form of the *be* verb (without the *to*) instead of the correct present form.

> Incorrect: They be good friends.
> Correct: They **are** good friends.
> Incorrect: Roberto be in my class.
> Correct: Roberto **is** in my class.

Activity D.   Find the mistake in each sentence. Write the sentences correctly.

1. "Where Roberto?" Stacy asked.
2. "He be at football practice," Sam said.
3. "They be practicing late today," she said.
4. "We be going to the drugstore after school."
5. "He be here soon," Sam told her.

●   The infinitive *to be* is not part of the verb or verb phrase. It it often used after the main verb.

> Donna appeared **to be** happy.
> Sam seems **to be** taller than Fred.
> I want **to be** the captain of the team.
> Donna tried **to be** friendly.

Lesson Review

Lesson Review.   Write these sentences on your paper. Write the correct form of the verb *to be* in each space.

1. In November there will _____ a contest at Wilson High School.
2. Jamie _____ entering the contest.
3. She wants to _____ "Miss Wilson High."
4. Her talent _____ playing the trumpet.
5. Sixty other girls _____ in the contest.
6. On the night of the contest, Jamie's parents _____ there.
7. Brad _____ in the front row.
8. Before the contest, Jamie had _____ nervous.
9. When she came on stage to play her trumpet, she _____ calm.
10. Later, she had to _____ in an evening gown.
11. She _____ wearing a bright red dress.
12. "Who will _____ the winner?" everyone wondered.
13. Finally, the judges announced the winner. Jamie _____ "Miss Wilson High."
14. Mr. and Mrs. Jones _____ very proud.
15. So _____ Brad.
16. Jamie _____ the happiest of all!

CHAPTER REVIEW

Part A.   Find the verb or verb phrase in each sentence. List all of them on your own paper.

1. The last days of November grew cold.
2. Winter winds felt chilly.
3. The days were growing shorter.
4. The sky became dark early in the evening.
5. The cool air smelled fresh and clean.
6. On most days the sky was clear.
7. There was little rain that fall.
8. Soon the first snowfall would come.
9. Everyone was feeling full of energy.
10. It was a pleasant time of the year.

Part B.   Decide whether the verb or verb phrase in each sentence expresses action or a state-of-being. Write your answers on your own paper.

1. The weather in December stayed cold.
2. People got out their winter coats.
3. "It gets cold earlier every year," Ron complained.
4. One day the sky looked gray.
5. "I can smell snow in the air," said Brad.
6. "It feels too cold to snow," Ron said.
7. "Hey! I felt a snowflake," said Brad.
8. They looked in Ron's garage for his sled.

Part C.   Write these sentences on your paper. Use the correct form of the verb *to be* in each.

1. "It definitely _____ snowing," Brad said.
2. "I _____ ready to go skiing," Ron said.
3. "So, now you _____ happy about the snow!"
4. Soon the snow _____ deep enough.
5. Ron and Brad _____ sledding on a nearby hill when it began to get dark.
6. They had _____ sledding for an hour.
7. They should _____ going home for dinner.
8. "I will _____ back soon!" said Brad.

CHAPTER 6

The Adverb

An *adverb* is a word that *modifies*, or answers questions about, a verb, an adjective, or another adverb.

- An adverb answers questions about the action or the state of being expressed in a sentence.

Questions	Examples
How?	Mr. Barrett drives **carefully**.
When?	The football game is **tomorrow**.
Where?	Sarah is studying **upstairs**.

- An adverb also answers questions about an adjective or another adverb. These adverbs are called adverbs of degree.

Questions	Examples
How bright?	A dolphin is **extremely** bright.
How small?	I had a **very** small lunch.
To what degree?	The winds howled **very loudly**.

Warm-Up A. Find the adverbs in the following sentences. Write them on your paper.

1. You should read the sentences carefully.
2. Adverbs are hidden everywhere.
3. The weather was very cold yesterday.
4. You are making too much noise.
5. I was almost asleep.
6. Julie threw her dog's old collar away today.

- *Never* and *not* are adverbs of negation. A negative word means that the action will not happen or that the state of being is not present. The adverb *not* is often hidden in a contraction.

  She is **never** home.
  My brother **won't** eat his dinner. (will not)
  They **didn't** find the book. (did not)
  Carol is **not** at school today.

Warm-Up B. Write these sentences on your own paper. Circle the adverbs of negation.

1. There is not enough snow to ski.
2. Fernando couldn't find his pencil.
3. It was not his fault.
4. I have never met him.
5. They had never been there before.

- Adverbs can be used to make comparisons. They are used much like adjectives. The words *more* and *most*, and *less* and *least,* are adverbs of degree. They are often used to compare adjectives or other adverbs.

Positive	Comparative	Superlative
fast	faster	fastest
slowly	more slowly	most slowly
quickly	less quickly	least quickly
well	better	best

Warm-Up C. For each sentence write the correct form of the adverb given in parentheses.

1. Of all the girls, Donna runs _____. (fast)
2. Howard works _____ than Jim. (slowly)
3. Beth sings well, but Dan sings _____ . (well)
4. When I am tired, I work _____ than when I am rested. (quickly)

Lesson 1. Adverbs That Modify Verbs

Adverbs that answer the question *How?* are usually used with action verbs. They tell us something about the way the action was done. Examples:

> The dog barked **loudly**.
> They did the assignment **correctly**.
> Jack guessed **right**.
> Carla works **quickly**.

Activity A. Write these sentences on your paper. Add an adverb that answers the question, "How was the action done?" The verb is in boldface.

1. The family **ate** their dinner..
2. Willis **drives** his car..
3. May **sews**..
4. **Read** these sentences..
5. Mrs. Barrett **sang**..
6. We **cleaned** the house..

Activity B. In each sentence, find the adverb that answers the question, *How?* Write the adverbs on your paper.

1. The ballerina danced gracefully.
2. The acrobat climbed the ladder carefully.
3. Laura helped us gladly.
4. Slowly Ella found the answers.
5. James played the game hard.
6. Sarah plays the trumpet well.
7. The farmer planted the corn quickly.
8. I got home fast.
9. We went on vacation happily.
10. She sewed the hem straight.

Adverbs also answer these questions: *When? How often? How long?* or *How many times?*

They tell something about the time of the action or state of being.

> I am leaving town **today**.
>
> Sarah will be home **soon**.
>
> I would like to go to the beach **again**.
>
> John will speak **next**.
>
> Carol is **usually** happy.

Adverbs also answer the question *Where?* or *In what direction?* They tell something about the place of the action or state of being.

> Brian lives **there**.
>
> Leave your coat **downstairs**.
>
> You should turn **left**.

Activity C.   Use each of these adverbs in a sentence. Underline each adverb.

1. often
2. tomorrow
3. never
4. still
5. yesterday
6. today
7. now
8. always
9. later
10. twice
11. already
12. again

Activity D. Each of these sentences has an adverb that tells something about the time of the action or state of being. List the adverbs on your paper.

1. Please begin immediately!
2. I'd like to go first.
3. They jumped up instantly.
4. That was a long time ago.
5. I saw the movie before.
6. The weather has been nice lately.
7. Sometimes I enjoy golf.
8. Occasionally we visit our relatives in Texas.
9. The newspaper is delivered daily.
10. We trim our trees yearly.

Activity E. Each sentence below has an adverb that tells something about the place of the action or state of being. List these adverbs on your paper.

1. The team advanced the ball forward.
2. Please go away.
3. Turn right at the corner.
4. Hang your coats here.
5. The bedrooms are upstairs.
6. They looked at the stars above.
7. The storm seems to be near.

Lesson Review

Lesson Review.   Read these sentences carefully. Find all of the adverbs. List them on your paper. A sentence may have more than one adverb.

1. Yesterday the dog carelessly lost his bone.
2. He barked loudly at Carla.
3. "You are always losing your things!" Carla scolded him angrily.
4. "I will never buy you anything again!"
5. Her dog jumped up and down constantly.
6. He would not stop barking.
7. Finally Carla found the bone.
8. She gave it to him quickly.
9. He ran away with it happily.
10. "Be careful with it now!" she reminded him.

Lesson 2. Adverbs of Degree

Adverbs that answer questions about adjectives and other adverbs are called adverbs of degree. They answer these questions: *How much? How little? How often?* and *To what degree?*

In this example, the adverb *very* tells us about the adjective *cold*.

It is **very** cold here.
How cold is it?
It is **very** cold!

In this example, the adverb *extremely* tells us about the adverb *fast*.

I work **extremely** fast.
How fast?
Extremely fast!

• The adverb of degree is usually placed before the adjective or adverb.

Activity A. Write these sentences on your own paper. Circle the adverbs of degree.

1. The dog is very careless.
2. He barks too much.
3. He makes everyone so angry!
4. He is an unusually noisy dog.

Activity B. Read these sentences. The boldfaced word is an adjective. Find the adverb that tells about the adjective. Write the adverb on your paper.

1. I am almost **ready** to go.
2. Fernando was rather **happy** today.
3. That coat is too **small** for you.
4. Mrs. Edwards was quite **pleased** with the class.
5. They were completely **satisfied** with their new stove.
6. The extremely **strong** wind blew down the tree.

Activity C. Read these sentences. The boldfaced word is an adverb. Find the word that tells something about the boldfaced adverb. Write it on your own paper.

1. Read these sentences very **carefully**.
2. Alissa works too **quickly**.
3. The band played unusually **well**.
4. I am leaving sometime **today**.
5. Please go far **away**.
6. Donna left much **later** than Yvonne.
7. Carlo swims somewhat **often**.

Activity D. Write these sentences on your own paper. Add an adverb of degree before the adjective or adverb that is in boldface. Use a different adverb of degree in each sentence.

1. The **strong** man lifted five hundred pounds.
2. Victor is **ready**.
3. Your new sweater is **pretty**.
4. Vanessa does her work **well**.
5. Anne plays tennis **often**.
6. Len works **quickly**.

Activity E. Use each of these adverbs of degree in a different sentence. Underline the adverb.

1. very	6. extremely
2. too	7. unusually
3. quite	8. completely
4. rather	9. so
5. somewhat	10. almost

Lesson Review

Part A. Read these sentences. Find the adverbs of degree. List them on your own paper.

1. Ray enjoyed his job at Mr. Jackson's store very much.
2. Mr. Jackson was completely satisfied with Ray's work.
3. Ray worked extremely hard.
4. "You are an unusually good worker," Mr. Jackson said.
5. "You can expect a very nice raise next month."
6. Ray was quite pleased to hear that!

Part B. In each of these sentences, find the adverb or adjective. Write the sentences on your paper. Add an adverb of degree to each one.

1. December is a cold month.
2. People must dress warmly.
3. Many of the trees are bare.
4. The skies may be cloudy.
5. Soon we will have snow.
6. I will be ready to go shopping tomorrow.

Lesson 3. Recognizing Adverbs

Sometimes people are not sure whether a word is an adjective or an adverb. Let's review the definitions of those two parts of speech.

- An adjective describes a noun or pronoun.

> Nancy is **tall**.
> Tall describes Nancy.
> *Nancy* is a noun; therefore, *tall* is an adjective.

- An adverb answers a question about a verb, an adjective, or another adverb in a sentence.

> Nancy lives **there**.
> There tells us where Nancy lives.
> *Lives* is a verb; therefore, *there* is an adverb.

Activity A. List the boldfaced words in these sentences. Next to each, write whether it is an adjective or an adverb.

1. Larry is **late**.
2. He is **here**.
3. That house is **large**.
4. She works **hard**.
5. He is a **hard** worker.
6. Jack lives **here**.
7. **Today** we jogged.
8. We arrived **late**.
9. They arrived **later**.
10. We **usually** eat at noon.
11. He runs **fast**.
12. He's a **fast** runner.
13. He is **fast**.
14. The answer is **clear**.
15. Speak **clearly**!
16. We shower **daily**.
17. Do **daily** exercises.
18. Let's go **early**.
19. Is this the **early** show?
20. We looked **up**.

- Many adverbs are made from adjectives by adding the ending *-ly*.

  Adjectives   **Adverbs**
  The cloth is **soft**.   He sang **softly**.
  The candy is **sweet**.   She smiled **sweetly**.
  Carol looks **happy**.   Fernando laughed **happily**.

- Sometimes an adverb is made from a noun by adding *-ly*.

  Noun   **Adverb**
  May I have **part** of that?   He is **partly** finished.

- Not all words ending in *-ly* are adverbs. Many common adjectives end in *-ly*, too.
  Examples:
      Ray received some **fatherly** advice from Mr. Barrett.
      Fatherly is an adjective that describes the noun *advice*.

      Donna is **usually friendly**.
      Friendly is an adjective that describes the noun *Donna*.

- Other words that end in *-ly* are used as either adjectives or adverbs.

  Adjectives   **Adverbs**
  He did the **daily** report.   He reported **daily**.
  We left in the **early** morning. We left **early**.

Activity B.   Write each boldfaced word. Tell whether it is an adjective or an adverb.

1. The sea was very **calm** today.
2. Donna walked **calmly** out of the room.
3. Between classes the halls were **quiet**.
4. The kangaroo **quietly** watched the people.
5. "This is an **extremely** difficult case," the lawyer said.
6. "This is an **extreme** case," the lawyer said.
7. Fernando is always **hungry**.
8. The people ate lunch **hungrily**.

Activity C.   Write each boldfaced word. Tell whether it is a noun or an adverb.

1. The books were in alphabetical **order**.
2. Please do things **orderly**.
3. We went to the store every **week**.
4. The family shops **weekly**.
5. The bills arrive every **month**.
6. We pay our bills **monthly**.

Activity D.   Is the boldfaced word in each sentence an adjective or an adverb? Write your answers on your own paper.

1. New cars are very **costly**.
2. Strychnine is a **deadly** poison.
3. That is an **ugly** cut.
4. They sat **quietly** and waited.
5. Donna's report was **timely**.

Lesson Review

Lesson Review. On your paper, identify the part of speech for each boldfaced word. List the words and write either *adjective* or *adverb* next to each.

1. We fed the rats a **deadly** poison.
2. Mr. Barrett prepared his **yearly** report.
3. We receive a newspaper **daily**.
4. Please try to come to class **early**.
5. Carla smiled **happily**.
6. Where have you been **lately**?
7. I am **partly** finished with my report.
8. They went to Chicago on the **early** train.
9. We listened to the **daily** weather report.
10. "The shoes this year are **ugly**," Sarah said.

Lesson 4. Comparing With Adverbs

Many adverbs are used to make comparisons. The three degrees of comparison are positive, comparative, and superlative.

Positive	Comparative	Superlative
fast	faster	fastest
slowly	more slowly	most slowly
happily	less happily	least happily
well	better	best

One-syllable adverbs form their comparative and superlative forms by adding -er and -est. Adverbs of more than one syllable usually form their comparative and superlative forms by using *more* and *most* and *less* and *least*. A few adverbs are irregular, such as *well, better, best.*

Remember to use the comparative form to compare two things. Use the superlative form to compare more than two things.

Donna finished **more** quickly than Ben.

Tom worked **most** quickly of them all.

Activity A.   On your paper, write the adverbs in the sentences below.

1. This shoe fits comfortably.
2. This shoe fits more comfortably than that one.
3. This shoe fits most comfortable of all.
4. Victor is speaking calmly.
5. He is speaking more calmly than George.
6. He speaks most calmly when he has practiced his speech.
7. Jack writes well.
8. He writes better this year.
9. He writes best about football.

Activity B.   Write each adverb below on your paper. Then write the comparative and superlative forms next to each.

Example:

> softly — **more softly, most softly**

1. loudly
2. brightly
3. fast
4. hard
5. gladly
6. clearly
7. softly
8. angrily

Activity C.   Write these sentences. Fill in the correct form of each adverb in parentheses.

1. The lights shone ____ . (brightly)
2. Carol sings ____ than Fernando. (well)
3. Dan works ____ when he is interested. (hard)
4. Of all the students, Kim worked ____ . (quickly)
5. Zeke played the trumpet ____ than Sarah. (loudly)

Lesson Review

Lesson Review.   Find the adverbs and list them on your paper. Write the degree of comparison beside each.

Example:

Sarah dances **most unusually**.
most unusually — superlative

1. Paul runs the mile faster than Sam.
2. Everyone in class worked hard.
3. I work best when I am rested.
4. Carl reads less quickly than Mike.
5. The choir sang the chorus more loudly than the verse.
6. Everyone worked least happily at the end of the day.
7. I like chocolate better than vanilla.
8. The winds howled most loudly at midnight.
9. The children played more quietly after lunch.
10. Sarah plays the trumpet well.

Lesson 5. Using Adverbs Correctly

Adverbs often tell us when the action in a sentence is taking place. *Ago* indicates past time. *Later* indicates future time. In a statement, the tense of the verb and the adverb of time must agree.

Incorrect: Jack **sings** next.
Correct: Jack **will sing** next.

Next suggests that the action will happen in the future. The verb should be future tense.

Incorrect: Tomorrow we **go** to work.
Correct: Tomorrow we **will go** to work.

Tomorrow is future time; therefore, the verb should be future tense.

Activity A.   In the sentences below, the adverbs of time are in boldface. Verbs are in parentheses. Write the correct tense of the verb for each sentence.

1. We ____ there a year **ago**. (go)
2. **Yesterday** we ____ late to class. (be)
3. Sally ____ **soon**. (arrive)
4. We ____ the house **before**. (paint)
5. Tiny ____ his dinner **now**. (eat)

Activity B.   Choose the correct word in parentheses after each sentence. Write it on your own paper.

1. Carol dances ____ . (graceful, gracefully)
2. Fernando laughed ____ . (happy, happily)
3. The winds howled ____ . (loud, loudly)
4. Give me that ____ ! (quick, quickly)
5. Sit there ____ ! (quiet, quietly)

• Use *good* and *well* correctly. *Good* is always an adjective and describes a noun. Never use *good* to answer questions about a verb.

Correct: We had a **good** day.
Incorrect: They worked **good** together. (tells *how* they worked)

Well is sometimes an adverb. *Well* means to do something correctly.

Correct: She speaks **well**. (tells *how* she speaks)
Incorrect: She speaks **good**.

Good and *well* can both be used after state-of-being verbs. In the sentence below, *well* is an adjective.

Correct: I feel **good** today. (describes emotions)
Correct: I feel **well** today. (describes health)

Activity C.   Write these sentences. Write either *good* or *well* in each space.

1. Carol is _____ at arithmetic.
2. Dan dances very _____ .
3. She did her _____ deed for the day.
4. Mike always does his work _____ .
5. Gail isn't feeling _____ today.

Lesson Review

Lesson Review.   Write the following sentences on your own paper. Correct the mistake with the adverb in each one.

1. Yesterday we are late to class.
2. Please finish that work quick.
3. Sarah plays the trumpet very good.
4. Between Fernando and Mike, Fernando drives best.
5. "Shhh! Sarah spoke now," said the teacher.
6. Anne always talks very soft.

CHAPTER REVIEW

In this chapter, your goal was to recognize adverbs in sentences. An adverb answers questions about verbs, adjectives, and other adverbs. The questions are *How? When? Where? How much? How often?* and *To what degree?*

Read these sentences. Find all of the adverbs. List them on your paper in order. A sentence may have more than one adverb.

1. A heavy snowfall arrived early in December.
2. Most of the people at Wilson High School were very happy.
3. The teachers and students waited somewhat patiently.
4. They were expecting an announcement that school would be dismissed early.
5. At home Ray was not so pleased.
6. He had to go to work anyway.
7. He knew the roads would be extremely slippery.
8. Mr. Jackson's store never closed for snow.
9. The store would probably be very busy.
10. The store was having an unusually good sale on ski jackets.
11. Ray drove more slowly that day.
12. Finally, he arrived at work.
13. He walked across the parking lot carefully.
14. The store was almost empty.
15. The other salespeople were talking excitedly about the snow.
16. The day passed quickly.
17. Soon it was time for Ray to leave.
18. "I still have time to go sledding," he thought to himself.
19. He found Sarah already outside.
20. "Hey! I'm here!" he called to her.

CHAPTER 7

The Preposition

A *preposition* is a word that shows a relationship between a noun or pronoun and another part of the sentence. A preposition is a part of a phrase.

The first word in the *prepositional phrase* is the preposition. The last word is the noun or pronoun. The noun or pronoun is called the object of the preposition.

Preposition   Object
We walked **through** the **woods**.

Examples:
down the street   for him
at the movies   under the table
in the middle   on the table

Warm-Up A. Read these sentences. Find the prepositional phrases and write them on your own paper.

1. My dog, Honey, saw another dog across the street.
2. The dog was sleeping under a tree.
3. Honey barked at the dog.
4. Then he dashed down the sidewalk.
5. He tried to play with the other dog.

• A prepositional phrase acts like an adjective or an adverb. It can describe nouns or verbs.
  Examples:

Adjective Phrases

The house **across the street** is for sale.
Which house? The one across the street.

The book **by Judy Blume** was popular.
Which book? The one by Judy Blume.

Adverb Phrases

Patrick works **in the evenings**.
When does Patrick work? In the evenings.

Please report **to the office**.
Report where? To the office.

Warm-Up B. Read these sentences. The prepositional phrases are in boldface. Decide if the phrase is an adjective or adverb. Write your answers on your paper.

1. The letter **from Mary** arrived yesterday.
2. The music **of Brahms** was played **at the concert**.
3. Patrick and Jeff both go **to Hanover Community College**.
4. Maria is a student **at Wilson High School**.
5. The gift **from my aunt** arrived **before Christmas**.
6. **During the winter** we like to ski.
7. Honey chased a cat **up a tree**.
8. A girl **in my class** wrote a short story.
9. She sent the story **to a magazine**.
10. The day **after tomorrow** is my birthday.

• Some words can be either a preposition or an adverb. A preposition has an object. An adverb does not.

    Preposition: She looked **up** the street.
                   Street is the object of the preposition *up*.
    Adverb: Jack looked **up**.

Warm-Up C. Read these sentences. Decide whether the boldfaced word is a preposition or an adverb. Write your answers on your own paper.

1. Please come **in**.
2. Howard walked **in** the woods.
3. Turn the lights **off** when you leave.
4. Jane jumped **off** the stage.
5. I will come **by** tomorrow.
6. Sam lives **by** the lake.
7. Mike came **over** to see us last night.
8. Honey jumped **over** the fence easily.

Lesson 1. Understanding Prepositions

A preposition expresses a relationship between a noun or a pronoun and another word in the sentence. That noun or pronoun is called the object of the preposition.

Examples:

Jan received a letter **from Mary**.

From is the preposition and expresses a relationship between Mary and a letter. *Mary* is the object of the preposition.

What is the relationship between the letter and Mary?
The letter is **from** Mary.

Jessie gave a book **to Stacy**.

To is the preposition and expresses a relationship between Stacy and a book. *Stacy* is the object of the preposition.

What is the relationship between the book and Stacy?
The book was given **to** Stacy.

Notice the differences between the following sentences.
The letter is **on** the box.
The letter is **under** the box.
The letter is **in** the box.

Activity A. Write each of these sentences on your paper. Write a word in the space that expresses a relationship between the two boldfaced words. Some sentences have more than one possible answer.

1. The **apples** _____ the **tree** are ripe.
2. The **house** _____ the **corner** is Jack's.
3. The **story** _____ **Edgar Allan Poe** was written in 1838.
4. The **girl** _____ the **picture** is my sister.
5. The **coat** _____ the **chair** is mine.
6. The **star** _____ the **movie** was John Wayne.
7. The **dessert** _____ **whipped cream** tasted best.
8. The **man** _____ the **beard** arrived late.
9. The **girl** _____ **Ken** is a good dancer.
10. The **picture** _____ the **wall** is my favorite.

• Each preposition has a certain meaning.

• A preposition must have an object. The object is a noun or pronoun.

        Preposition + object = prepositional phrase

• The object of a preposition may have adjectives in front of it.
        across **the muddy** field

• Because adverbs answer questions about adjectives, a prepositional phrase may also contain an adverb.
        after the **very** long meeting

• When the object of the preposition is a pronoun, the prepositional phrase will usually be only two words — the preposition and the object.
        to him   for her   beside it

Activity B. Here is a list of some commonly used prepositions. Write a sentence using each one. Underline the whole prepositional phrase. Example:

aboard— Fred is <u>aboard the ship</u>.

1. about	8. behind	15. in	22. over
2. above	9. beneath	16. into	23. past
3. across	10. beside	17. near	24. through
4. after	11. down	18. of	25. to
5. around	12. during	19. off	26. under
6. at	13. for	20. on	27. until
7. before	14. from	21. out	28. with

Activity C. Read these sentences. Find the prepositional phrases. Write them on your own paper.

1. We bought our groceries at the store.
2. Here is a list of sentences.
3. We looked across the clear blue lake.
4. We lived near a very busy highway.
5. Would you please sit here with me?
6. Write your name in the left-hand corner.
7. Give this book to him.
8. Around the corner lives my best friend.
9. I like apple pie with ice cream.
10. John Kelly was mayor of the city.
11. Did you vote for him?
12. James Polk was born in North Carolina.
13. Later Polk moved to Tennessee.
14. Susan walked home during a heavy storm.
15. Howard gave this gift to me.

• Some words can be either a preposition or an adverb. A preposition has an object. An adverb does not.

Jim looked **around**.

Around is an adverb. *Around* tells where Jim looked.

Jim looked **around** the corner.

Around is a preposition. *Around* expresses a relationship between its object (*corner*) and the rest of the sentence.

Activity D. Read each sentence. Decide whether the boldfaced word is a preposition or an adverb. Write your answers on your paper.

1. Colleen put Honey **outside**.
2. Honey barked **outside** the door.
3. Don't stay **outside** in the rain.
4. Put the cat **out**!
5. Turn the light **out** before you leave.
6. Quick! Come look **out** the window!
7. The rain was falling **down** heavily.
8. We drove the car **down** the highway.

Activity E. Use each of the words below in two sentences. Use it first as a preposition. Then use it as an adverb.

1. in
2. on
3. below
4. up
5. underneath
6. inside

- Compound prepositions are made up of more than one word.
  Examples:

according to	in spite of
because of	instead of
in addition to	out of
in front of	as far as
in place of	along with

Activity F.   Find the compound preposition in each sentence. Write the whole prepositional phrase on your paper.

Example: John stood in front of Maria. — in front of Maria

1. According to Joe, the party was fun.
2. I am going instead of Tim.
3. Vic will speak in place of Judy.
4. Please get the dog out of the house.
5. Randy will go along with us.
6. Donna is in front of Karl.

Lesson Review

Lesson Review.   Read these sentences. Find all of the prepositional phrases. Make a list of them on your paper.

1. Patrick was studying for his final exams.
2. He stayed in his room and studied.
3. Jeff called him on the telephone.
4. "I need some help from you," he said.
5. Jeff lived around the corner.
6. He arrived in ten minutes.
7. "It is math again," he said. "It is just too tough for me."
8. In spite of his troubles, Jeff passed the test.

Lesson 2. The Prepositional Phrase Used as an Adjective

The prepositional phrase is usually used in a sentence either as an adjective phrase or as an adverb phrase. In this lesson you will study the adjective phrase.

An adjective is a word that describes or defines a noun or pronoun. A prepositional phrase can be used as an adjective. The prepositional phrase used as an adjective does the same thing as an adjective. The phrase tells *which one*, *what kind*, or *how many*.

You will notice that the adjective usually comes before the noun. The prepositional phrase comes after the noun. Both sentences have the same meaning.

Adjective: The **middle** girl is Jean.
Prepositional Phrase: The girl **in the middle** is Jean.

Adjective: The **Wilson High** team won.
Prepositional Phrase: The team **from Wilson High** won.

Activity A.   The boldfaced words in these sentences are prepositional phrases. Find the word that each phrase is describing. Write it on your paper.

Example: What kind **of car** is that?   kind

1. Jeff's homework **in math** was difficult.
2. The boy **with me** is my cousin.
3. The flowers **on the table** are beautiful.
4. We built a house **of brick**.
5. None **of the girls** left early.
6. All **of the people** applauded.
7. The poem **by Emily Dickinson** was lovely.

Activity B.   Rewrite each of these sentences. Change the adjective in boldface to a prepositional phrase.

1. **John Steinbeck's** story was exciting to read.
2. Colleen bought **football** tickets.
3. It was a beautiful **spring** day.
4. We chose a lovely **diamond** ring.
5. I bought a **city** map.
6. The **porch** light needed a new bulb.
7. Those are **ski** boots.
8. The **kitchen** table is new.
9. Carol's **English** homework was easy.
10. We built a **brick** house.

- A prepositional phrase can describe the object of another preposition.
  >The man **at the end of the line** is Mr. Jones.
  >*At the end* describes man; *of the line* tells about end.

- Prepositional phrases used as adjectives make sentences more interesting.

Activity C.   Find all of the prepositional phrases in these sentences. Write them on your own paper.

1. We walked in the woods beside the lake.
2. Patrick works in a store in Marshall Mall.
3. We went to Yellowstone Park in Wyoming.
4. Put this on the table in your room.
5. All of the people in the auditorium cheered.

Activity D.   Rewrite these sentences. Add a prepositional phrase after each noun or pronoun.

1. **Everyone** likes the football **games**.
2. Several **people** are coming to the **party**.
3. The **books** fell off the **shelf**.
4. The **library** closed at **noon**.
5. The **man** bought a new **car**.
6. The **teacher** liked that **book**.

Lesson Review

Lesson Review.   Find the prepositional phrases in these sentences. List them on your paper. After the phrase write the word it is describing. Example:

> The pen **on Frank's desk** has no ink.
> **on Frank's desk** — pen

1. Alaska in January is very cold.
2. The beautiful spruces throughout the state are snow-covered.
3. Maria studied the history of Alaska.
4. Vitus Bering was the first explorer of Alaska.
5. People from Russia also explored there.
6. The Russians made their headquarters in Sitka.
7. Now Alaska is a state in the United States.
8. Alaska is one of our last frontiers.
9. The population of Alaska is very small.
10. Maria enjoyed her study of Alaska.

Lesson 3. The Prepositional Phrase Used as an Adverb

An adverb is a word that answers questions about a verb. A prepositional phrase can also be used as an adverb.

Adverb: We shopped **rapidly**.

Prepositional Phrase: We shopped **in a hurry**.

The prepositional phrase used as an adverb does the same thing as an adverb. The phrase tells us *how* we shopped.

- A prepositional phrase also answers the question *why*?
  Example:

    Maria bought a gift for her mother's birthday.
    Why did Maria buy the gift?

Activity A.   The prepositional phrase in each sentence is an adverb phrase. Decide what question the adverb phrase is answering about the verb. On your paper, write *How*, *When*, or *Where* for each sentence.

1. I will be there **in a minute**.
2. Colleen ran **up the stairs**.
3. Jeff and Patrick drove **to the lake**.
4. The report was written **before midnight**.
5. Shakespeare was born **in 1564**.
6. We are going **to Florida**.
7. Make the pudding **with milk**.
8. Maria ironed her dress **with great care**.
9. The roast is **in the oven**.
10. Write your paragraph **in ink**.
11. Karl took his car **to the garage**.
12. Mr. Jones drives **on Route 50** every day.
13. They went **to the beach** last summer.
14. She did her work **with a smile**.
15. Park the car **in the garage**.

Activity B. Each of these sentences has an adverb phrase. The phrase tells *why* something was done. List the adverb phrases on your paper.

1. I took an umbrella because of the rain.
2. Maria wrote a paper for English class.
3. Mrs. Jones made dinner for her family.
4. She bought an onion for the salad.
5. Patrick bought a car for himself.
6. Please do something for me.
7. Jeff took an aspirin because of his fever.

• A prepositional phrase used as an adverb answers a question about the verb. The phrase may tell something about the conditions of the action.

    Examples:

    Colleen went **there** with Maria.
    Colleen was *with Maria* when she went there.

    Fred is now taller **by three inches**.
    How much taller is Fred? He is taller by three inches. The prepositional phase, *by three inches*, tells something about the adjective *taller*.

    In the race, Dan ran faster than Jack **by eight seconds**.
    How much faster than Jack did Dan run? He ran faster by eight seconds. The prepositional phrase, *by eight seconds*, tells something about the adverb *faster*.

Activity C. Find the prepositional phrases in these sentences. They will all be used as adverbs. A sentence may have more than one prepositional phrase. Write them on your own paper.

1. Put the paper in the trash can.
2. The office is on the first floor of the building.
3. She was with her mother at the store.
4. Carol shopped for the family's groceries.
5. The firefighters saved the family from the fire.

Activity D. Write these sentences on your paper. Add a prepositional phrase which answers a question about the boldfaced word. (*How? When? Where? By how much?*)
Example:

> I **saw** Tim.
> Where did I see Tim?
> I saw Tim **at school**.

1. Sally weighs **more** than Cathy.
2. Zack **walks** every day.
3. They **arrived**.
4. Maria **took** her coat.
5. Patrick **drove** his car.
6. The winds **blew** very hard.
7. Bob got the **highest** grade on the test.
8. We **visited** my aunt.
9. Please **fix** dinner.
10. Frank **did** his homework.

Lesson Review

Lesson Review.   Remember that the prepositional phrase begins with a preposition. It ends with a noun or pronoun. Find the prepositional phrases in these sentences. List them on your paper in order.

1. Jeff is a student at Hanover Community College.
2. He will study computer technology for two years.
3. He will also take courses in accounting.
4. Someday Jeff may work in a bank.
5. Computer workers are in almost every industry.
6. The first computers were installed in business firms in 1951.
7. Now, almost every business uses computers for recordkeeping.
8. At school, Jeff loads computers with diskettes or tapes.
9. He watches the screen for information.
10. Jeff is also learning about computer languages.
11. A computer programmer works with computer languages.
12. The programmer writes directions for the computer.
13. So far, Jeff enjoys his work with computers.
14. He hopes to have a good job in this field.

Lesson 4. The Object of the Preposition

The object of the preposition is a noun or a pronoun. Be sure that you do not confuse a prepositional phrase with an infinitive. The word after the *to* in an infinitive is a verb. A prepositional phrase never includes a verb.

Examples:

Infinitives:	He wants **to leave** early.
	He hopes **to have** a job.
Prepositional Phrases:	Patrick went **to the bank**.
	Maria wrote a letter **to her aunt**.

Activity A.   Read each sentence. Decide whether the boldfaced words are an infinitive or a prepositional phrase. Write your answers on your paper.

1. Jeff went **to his class**.
2. He likes **to work** with computers.
3. "Turn **to page 8**," the teacher said.
4. Jeff began **to read** his lesson.
5. He wanted **to ask** the teacher a question.
6. He went **to the computer to practice**.
7. Patrick sent a get-well card **to his friend**.
8. The girl ran **to catch** the bus.
9. People on the bus waved **to her**.
10. Colleen climbed **to the top** of a high hill.

Activity B.   Write five sentences using the word *to*. Decide whether *to* is part of a prepositional phrase or part of an infinitive in each of your sentences.

- The object of the preposition must be a noun or a pronoun. If it is a pronoun, it must be in the objective case.

    Incorrect: She sat between Patrick and **I**.

    Correct: She sat between Patrick and **me**.

- Possessive nouns and pronouns are NOT used as objects of prepositions.

    Incorrect: Jack went home with **his**.

    Correct: Jack went home with **him**.

                                OR

                Jack went home with **his friend**.

Activity C.   Read these sentences. Find the prepositional phrases. List them on your paper.

1. Colleen wanted to study with her friend.
2. The table was empty. I put my books on it.
3. Patrick studied by himself.
4. We bought gifts for everyone.
5. They had to choose between them.
6. Marty asked, "May I have a salad with this?"

Activity D.   Write these sentences on your paper.   Correct any mistakes.

1. Please bring a coat for Jack and I.
2. Sam bought a soda for hisself.
3. Susan passed out paper to everyone's.
4. Between the two of those, I like the red sweater better.

- The object of a preposition usually comes after the preposition. However, sometimes the preposition and its object are separated in sentences that ask questions.

  Object   Preposition

  What did you do that **for?**

Activity E.   Find the preposition and its object in each sentence. Write the whole phrase on your paper.

1. Whom are you talking about?
2. Whom are Howard and Tom with?
3. I found the pen that he was writing with.
4. Patrick found the book that he was looking for.
5. That is what I was searching for.

Activity F.   Read the paragraph below. Find all of the prepositional phrases and list them on your paper. There are three infinitives that should not be on your list.

Have you ever heard of Mary Lyon? She was a pioneer in the education of women. Mary Lyon was born in 1797. She died in 1849. She taught in schools in New Hampshire and in Massachusetts. In those days, only rich women could get a good education. She raised money to begin a school for middle-class women. In 1837, she opened a school in Massachusetts. The name of the school was Mount Holyoke. There women studied about mathematics, science, and Latin. Mary Lyon had no goal except to teach. She won the love of everyone through her work. Mary Lyon wanted to give women confidence in themselves.

Lesson Review

Lesson Review.   Find the prepositional phrases in these sentences.
List them on your own paper.

1. Jeff hopes to have a job in a bank.
2. He likes to work with computers.
3. Jeff had to study for a test.
4. He studied with Patrick and Mike.
5. The teacher gave the test to everyone.
6. They had no choice except to concentrate hard.
7. They had prepared for the test by studying.
8. Jeff made a mistake on his paper.
9. "What did I do that for?" he thought.
10. Finally, he was finished with the test.
11. He gave his paper to the teacher and breathed a sigh of relief.

CHAPTER REVIEW

Part A.   A prepositional phrase in each of these sentences is in boldface. Decide whether it is used as an adverb or an adjective.

1. The dress **in the window** is on sale.
2. The letter **from Aunt Sue** arrived yesterday.
3. Carol waited **for the mail carrier**.
4. **In the spring** we plant a garden.
5. I mowed the lawn **for my neighbor**.

Part B.   Read these sentences. Find all of the prepositional phrases. List them on your paper in order.

1. Mike came to see me for a minute.
2. He arrived in a yellow sports car.
3. We invited him to stay for dinner.
4. Mother made pizza for everyone.
5. Later we all helped with the clean-up.

Part C.   Write these sentences on your paper. Add at least one prepositional phrase to each one.

1. Everyone was happy.
2. The weather was good.
3. The family went out.
4. They came home.
5. The family was tired.

CHAPTER 8

The Conjunction

A *conjunction* is a word that connects parts of a sentence. They can connect words, phrases, or ideas.

Words: Becky **and** Lisa went to the game.
Spaghetti sauce needs tomatoes, onions, **and** spices.

Phrases: The basketball team got the ball **and** scored a goal.
Jack ran around the corner **and** down the street.

Ideas: Anthony looked at new cars, **but** they were too expensive.
He liked the big cars best; **however**, he wanted good gas mileage.

Some conjunctions also introduce groups of words called subordinate clauses. They answer the questions *where, when, how,* and *why.*

Because Shelly was late, she missed the bus.
Why did she miss the bus?

She had to walk **if** she wanted to get to school.
Why did she have to walk?

Other conjunctions come in pairs.
Examples:

Neither Marco **nor** Anthony caught a fish.
Either Brian **or** Carrie will lead the group.

• Conjunctions may be used to connect several ideas into one sentence.

Lisa is in line. Becky is in line. Todd is in line. Others are in line.
Lisa, Becky, Todd, and others are in line.

Warm-Up A. Read these sentences. Find the conjunctions. List them on your own paper.

1. The football team scored the touchdown and the extra point.
2. Would you like vanilla or chocolate pudding?
3. Jack will succeed if he keeps on trying.
4. I would like to go, but I am tired.
5. We missed school yesterday because it was snowing.
6. Carol likes hockey; however, she prefers tennis.
7. Either tea or coffee will be fine.
8. For my birthday I got not only skis but also ski poles.
9. Alice didn't know whether to laugh or cry.
10. Becky, Lisa, and Todd are in the same class.
11. Fran checked the book out, but Dan read it.
12. We bought meat, fruit, and milk at the store.
13. After the game was over, the school had a dance.
14. Unless you try harder, you will not win.

Warm-Up B. Rewrite these sentences. Use a conjunction to connect the ideas.

1. Paul bought a coat. He bought a scarf. He bought some gloves.
2. It rained on Monday. It rained on Tuesday.
3. Dan was absent. Abby was absent.

Lesson 1. Coordinating Conjunctions

There are three kinds of conjunctions: the *coordinating conjunction*, the *subordinating conjunction*, and the *correlative conjunction*.

A *coordinating conjunction* connects words, phrases, or sentences that do not depend on each other to make sense.
Examples:

> Shoes **and** boots are on sale today.
> You could express this in two sentences.
> Shoes are on sale today. Boots are on sale today.

Words: Rich plays the guitar **and** the trumpet.

Phrases: He ran around the corner **and** out of sight.

Ideas: I'd like to help you, **but** I'm busy.

Some of the most common coordinating conjunctions are: *and, but, or, for, nor, as well as,* and *yet.*

Activity A. Find the coordinating conjunction in each sentence. Write it on your paper.

1. Eight and eight make sixteen.
2. All night the winds blew, and the snow fell.
3. The referee blew his whistle and stopped the game.
4. The actor sang well, but he could not dance.
5. I don't like tea or coffee.
6. I couldn't study, for I was so tired.

• A coordinating conjunction may connect two or more complete ideas.

We can say: I don't like tea. I don't like coffee.

We can also say: I don't like tea **or** coffee.

The words that are the same in both sentences are not repeated.

Activity B. Connect the ideas in the following pairs of sentences, using conjunctions. You may need to change the verb form.

1. Carol likes ice cream. Lance likes ice cream.
2. Todd plays football. Todd plays baseball.
3. Edgar Allan Poe wrote short stories. Edgar Allan Poe wrote poetry.
4. I grew tomatoes in my garden. I grew green beans in my garden.
5. Laura likes basketball. Laura likes hockey.

Activity C. Rewrite each of these sentences into two sentences. Leave out the conjunctions.

Example:
                 We bought hamburgers **and** rolls.
                 We bought hamburgers. We bought rolls.

1. I like milk or water with my dinner.
2. Lance hits well, but he cannot catch a ball.
3. Vic tried hard but couldn't make the team.
4. Poe wrote short stories as well as poetry.
5. After school we played records and relaxed.
6. John Adams and Thomas Jefferson were vice-presidents of the United States.
7. President Harry Truman was born in 1884 and died in 1972.

- Use a comma to separate words or phrases in a series. A series is three or more words or phrases. Place the comma after each item in the series. Do not put a comma after the last item in the series. Examples:

     Lisa and Becky arrived late.
     (Only two people — do not use commas)

     Lisa, Becky, and Sue arrived late.
     (Three people — use commas)

     We planted flowers in the front, in the back, and on the sides of the house.
     (Three phrases — use commas)

Activity D.   Write these sentences on your paper. Add commas only where they are needed. Circle the conjunctions.

1. We planted bushes trees and flowers around the house.
2. We planted tulips daffodils and hyacinths.
3. Later we washed up changed our clothes and went out to dinner.
4. I ordered a hamburger french fries and milk.
5. For dessert we had a choice of ice cream pie cake or pudding.
6. The restaurant had vanilla ice cream but no strawberry.
7. They had apple cherry and peach pie.

Activity E.   Write a sentence using each of these conjunctions. Each sentence should have a series. Be sure to punctuate the series correctly.

1. and   4. nor
2. but   5. as well as
3. or   6. for

- Two or more sentences joined with a conjunction usually need a punctuation mark. Use a comma to separate sentences joined with *and, but, nor, or, for.*
  Examples:

   Marco dug up the garden, **and** Leslie planted the seeds.
   Our family doesn't like spinach, **nor** do we like squash.

Some sentences are too short to require punctuation. No comma is required before *and* because the sentence is too short.
Examples:

   We went out and then we went home.
   She is tall and he is short.

When you join complete sentences with these connectives, use a semicolon (;) in front of them and a comma (,) after them.

besides	however	furthermore
accordingly	also	therefore
moreover	otherwise	consequently
nevertheless	instead	

Examples:

   Lisa likes to play the piano; **however**, she doesn't like to practice.
   Lance worked all day; **nevertheless**, he didn't finish.

- The words *but* and *for* can be used either as conjunctions or as prepositions.

Conjunction: Becky feeds her puppy dog food, **but** he prefers steak!

Preposition: No one was hungry **but** Timmy.

Conjunction: Randy brought the equipment, **for** he was the team manager.

Preposition: We knew that he would bring it **for** the team.

Activity F.   Write these sentences on your paper. Punctuate them correctly.

1. Lisa must hurry otherwise she will be late.
2. We wanted to go shopping instead we stayed home.
3. After dinner Lisa read a book Marco did homework Mr. Martin watched TV and Mrs. Martin just relaxed.
4. Karl rode the bus to school but he walked home.
5. Tiny likes steak but all he gets is dog food.
6. The storm blew down several trees furthermore it damaged some telephone lines.
7. Poe wrote many stories also he wrote some good poetry.
8. Roberto likes ice cream but his sister served pudding for dessert.

Activity G.   Read these sentences carefully. Identify the part of speech of the boldfaced word.

1. Paul played tennis well, **for** he practiced every day.
2. The new apartment was beautiful, **but** the rent was high.
3. Everyone liked the story **but** Yolanda.
4. The students cheered loudly **for** their team.

Lesson Review

Lesson Review.   Write these sentences on your paper. Add the necessary punctuation. Circle the coordinating conjunctions.

1. A new girl moved to the town where Lisa and Becky live.
2. Her name is Antoinette but everyone calls her Toni.
3. Toni was shy at first for she is deaf.
4. Lisa and Becky wanted to communicate with Toni better therefore they began to study sign language.
5. Soon they could use signs or finger spelling easily.
6. Sign language helped them "talk" to Toni furthermore it was fun!

Lesson 2. Subordinating Conjunctions

A *subordinating conjunction* connects one complete idea with an incomplete idea or dependent clause. A dependent clause is a group of words with a subject and a verb, but it does not express a complete idea. The dependent clause cannot stand alone as a sentence. It does not express a complete thought by itself. The clause introduced by the subordinating conjunction depends upon the main clause (the independent idea) to make sense. Like an adverb, dependent clauses answer the questions *when*, *where*, *why*, and *how*.

Examples:

If the rain stops.

What will happen? The thought is incomplete.

If the rain stops, we can start practice.

- The dependent clause may be found at the beginning or the end of the sentence. Use a comma after the dependent clause only when it is at the beginning of the sentence.

Comma: **Unless you hurry**, you won't finish.
             After the party was over, we went home.

No comma: You won't finish **unless you hurry**.
             We went home **after the party was over**.

Here is a list of some commonly used subordinating conjunctions:

after	if	until
although	since	when
as	so	where
because	unless	while
whenever	wherever	in order that

Activity A. Find the dependent clause in each sentence. Write it on your paper. Include the subordinating conjunction that begins each dependent clause.

1. If you are gaining weight, skip dessert.
2. I plan to study until I finish.
3. Justin's parents saved their money in order that he could go to college.
4. When Lisa gets here, we will leave.
5. They ate popcorn while they watched the movie.
6. Newton is ten miles away as the crow flies.

Activity B. Add an independent clause (a complete sentence) to each of these dependent clauses.

1. Although Benji is only a dog,
2. Until the other team scored,
3. Because my tooth aches,
4. Since I flew on an airplane,
5. When I finish this book,

Activity C. Now add a dependent clause to each of these sentences. Write the complete new sentence on your paper. Circle the subordinating conjunction that begins each dependent clause.

1. Dan would like to visit California.
2. Karl saved five dollars a week.
3. My neighbors got a new dog.
4. Anne's report was always late.
5. The Martin family might buy a computer.

Activity D. Connect each of these pairs of sentences with a subordinating conjunction. Punctuate your sentences correctly.

1. Zack is lifting weights. He wants to be on the wrestling team.
2. Pete went to the library. He needed a book.
3. Sue is in Becky's English class. She moved to town in March.
4. I was asleep. A storm blew down our tree.
5. You will drive today. I will drive tomorrow.

- Some words can be used either as subordinating conjunctions or as prepositions.

    Conjunction: The game stopped **because** it rained.

    Preposition: The game stopped **because of** rain.

In the first example, *it rained* is a clause. It has a subject and a verb. In the second example, *rain* is the object of the preposition *because of*. Remember that prepositional phrases never include verbs.

Activity E. Read each sentence. Decide whether the boldfaced word is a conjunction or a preposition. Write your answers on your own paper.

1. Donna went home **after** school.
2. We went home **after** school was over.
3. **Because of** Marco, we won the game.
4. I like that coat **because** it is warm.
5. I haven't heard from her **since** Monday.
6. I'll leave **since** you are here now.
7. **Before** class began, I talked to the teacher.
8. **Before** lunch, I have my French class.

Activity F. Find the subordinating conjunctions in these sentences. List them on your own paper.

1. We drove home carefully because it was snowing.
2. We had classes until noon although the weather was bad.
3. If the snow is deep enough, there will be no school tomorrow.
4. School is closed only when the snow is deep.
5. Where Lisa and Marco live, there are usually two deep snows each year.

Lesson Review

Part A. Connect each of these pairs of sentences with a subordinating conjunction. Punctuate the new sentence correctly. Be sure that your new sentence makes sense.

1. I got an A. I studied hard.
2. I will clean the house. You do the shopping.
3. I get hungry about three o'clock. I eat an apple.
4. The weather is too cold. I can't go outside.
5. He lost the election. He didn't get enough votes.

Part B. Write these sentences on your paper. Add the necessary punctuation. Circle the subordinating conjunctions. If this conjunction begins the sentence, add a comma after the dependent clause.

1. Kathy won't fix dinner until everyone is hungry.
2. If you will help we can finish early.
3. When warm weather arrives Marco and Anthony will go fishing.
4. Until the team scored the fans were quiet.
5. Everyone looked forward to warmer weather as spring approached.

Lesson 3. Correlative Conjunctions

Correlative conjunctions are always used in pairs.
Examples:

> **Neither** Marco **nor** Anthony enjoyed that movie.
> **Both** the actors **and** the story were awful!

Here is a list of the most common pairs of correlative conjunctions:

> neither.... nor
> both.... and
> not only... but also
> either... or
> whether... or

Activity A.   Read these sentences. Find the correlative conjunctions.
Write them on your own paper.

1. Ann Marie will write her report on either James Polk or Benjamin
    Harrison.
2. Both Polk and Harrison were U.S. presidents.
3. Not only Ann Marie but also Susan must write a report.
4. Neither Polk nor Harrison is very famous.
5. Susan doesn't know whether to write about Chester Arthur or
    Franklin Pierce.
6. She had heard of neither Arthur nor Pierce before.

- When subjects are joined with correlative conjunctions, the verb agrees with the subject nearest the verb.

Incorrect: **Neither** Justin **nor** Mark are home yet.
Correct: **Neither** Justin **nor** Mark is home yet.
               (*Mark* is singular.)

Incorrect: **Not only** the house **but also** the garage need painting.
Correct: **Not only** the house **but also** the garage needs painting.
               (*Garage* is singular.)

Incorrect: **Either** candy **or** flowers is a nice gift.
Correct: **Either** candy **or** flowers are a nice gift.
               (*Flowers* is plural.)

Activity B.   Choose the correct word in the parentheses to complete each sentence.

1. Either a pencil or a pen ____ satisfactory. (is, are)
2. Neither the coat nor the shoes ____ on sale. (is, are)
3. Neither the car nor the truck ____ working today. (is, are)
4. Not only Jack but also Kristen ____ running for class president. (is, are)
5. Either candy or perfume ____ a nice gift. (makes, make)

Lesson Review

Lesson Review.   Find the correlative conjunctions in these sentences. Write them on your own paper.

1. Both Mark and Justin have part-time jobs.
2. Susan takes neither cream nor sugar in her coffee.
3. Not only Becky but also her St. Bernard enjoys "Benji."
4. Mr. Martin either drives to work or takes the bus.
5. Mr. Wiley must decide whether the reports are due on Monday or Tuesday.

CHAPTER REVIEW

Conjunctions are words that connect two or more words, phrases, or ideas in a sentence.

Part A.   Read these sentences.   Find all of the conjunctions. List them on your paper.

1. Lisa and Becky were making plans for the Valentine's Day dance.
2. Becky wondered whether Todd would ask her or not.
3. She decided to buy a new dress when she got her next paycheck.
4. Lisa wanted to ask Anthony, but she wasn't sure if he would go.
5. She also wasn't sure if Marco would approve.
6. After a few days passed, Lisa got the courage.
7. "Either he will or he won't," she thought.
8. Anthony did want to go, but he had a problem.
9. "I have neither money nor a good suit," he said.
10. "If you just wear slacks and a sports shirt, you will look fine," Lisa told him.
11. "If it's that simple, I will go," said Anthony.
12. Lisa was pleased because he would be her date.

Part B.   Write these sentences on your paper. Add the necessary punctuation.

1. Lisa Anthony Becky and Todd went to the dance together.
2. Because the car was small they were somewhat crowded.
3. While they were on their way they had a good time.
4. "If we don't get there soon we will miss the first dance," Becky said.
5. "The dance committee wanted a band however they got a disc jockey," Lisa said.
6. When they arrived they hurried to join their friends.
7. "Shall we dance or shall we check out the food," Anthony asked.
8. "Unless you're hungry let's dance," she answered.
9. The music was good and they had a wonderful evening.

Part C.   Write these sentences on your paper. Fill in each space with a conjunction. There may be more than one correct answer.

1. ____ the dance, they went to a restaurant.
2. They were hungry,____ they were not tired.
3. ____ Todd ____ Anthony ordered hamburgers.
4. "I'm on a diet," said Lisa; " ____, I will have a milkshake."
5. They talked to the disc jockey ____ their friends.
6. ____ it was time to go home, they got back into the car.
7. Guess who was waiting ____ Anthony took Lisa to her door!
8. ____ were her parents there, ____ there was also Marco!

CHAPTER 9

The Interjection

An *interjection* is a word or phrase that expresses feeling. An interjection is not clearly related to the rest of the sentence. The interjection is a word that is "thrown in." It is not essential to the meaning of the sentence.

Examples:

> **Oh, no!** I forgot my money.
> **Ah, yes**, this is terrific.
> **What?** You don't know how to land this plane?

The interjection is always separated from the rest of the sentence with a punctuation mark. You can use a comma, a question mark, or an exclamation point. Use an exclamation point after a strong interjection.

> **Hurray!** We finally won the game.
> **Help! Fire! Please hurry!**

Warm-Up. Read the following sentences. Write each sentence on your paper. Add an interjection. Be sure to punctuate correctly.

1. Isn't that beautiful?
2. We're having a test.
3. That hurts.
4. I ripped my best shirt.
5. I won!
6. We're having liver.

Lesson 1. Using Interjections

An interjection is a word or phrase that expresses a strong feeling. Always separate the interjection from the rest of the sentence with a punctuation mark.

Examples:
> **Oh, no!** I'm late again.
> **Oh?** I didn't know you were sick.
> **Hush.** Everyone is working.
> **Say,** could you help me?

Here are some other commonly used interjections:

Yes.	Whew!	Gosh.	My goodness!
Hey!	What?	Ha!	Nonsense!
Ah.	Ouch!	Hurry!	Oh, boy.
Well.	Wow!	So what?	Really?
Hello.	Quick!	Sorry.	Alas!

Activity A.   Make a list of ten different interjections. Include either words or short phrases. Use each one in a sentence. Be sure to punctuate correctly.

- Capitalize the first word of the sentence after a mark of end punctuation such as a period, a question mark, or an exclamation point.

> So? Who really cares?
> Wow! That is lovely.
> Whew. I'm glad I am finished!

- You can also use a comma after an interjection. Do not capitalize the first word of the sentence that follows the comma.

> Ah, that dessert looks great!

Activity B.   Write these sentences on your paper. Add punctuation after the interjections and at the end of the sentences. Capitalize the first words of sentences.

1. quick I need help fast
2. oh boy what a great car
3. really I didn't know that
4. well you finally got here
5. oh no you aren't giving me a shot

CHAPTER REVIEW

Chapter Review.   Write 10 sentences using interjections. Be sure to capitalize the first word of sentences and use proper punctuation.

PART II

SENTENCE STRUCTURE

What Is a Sentence?

A sentence is a group of words containing a subject and a predicate that expresses a complete thought. A sentence may be very short. Some of the ideas we wish to express are very simple. Other sentences may be very long because some of our ideas are complicated. The most important rule to remember about a sentence is that it should communicate a complete idea to another person.

- A sentence must express a complete idea.
- A sentence has a subject and a predicate. The subject names the person or thing that we are talking about. The predicate tells us what happened. The predicate always includes a verb.

Activity A. Listed below are groups of words. Write them on your paper. State whether or not each group of words forms a sentence.

1. Stop!
2. Before the storm was over.
3. Across the street.
4. That's nice.
5. Every sentence expresses a complete idea.
6. Looking at new cars.
7. She laughed.
8. Jack thought that he would like to go fishing, but because of the cold weather he stayed home.

- The subject is usually a noun or pronoun. The words that describe the subject are part of the complete subject. We call the noun or pronoun by itself the simple subject.

    Simple subject: Sam's **car** had a flat tire.
    Complete subject: **Sam's car** had a flat tire.

• The predicate part of a sentence tells us what happened. The predicate always includes a verb. All of the words that tell about the verb are part of the complete predicate.

Activity B. Write these sentences on your paper. Underline the subject once and the predicate twice.

1. Andy is looking at new cars.
2. Everyone at the party had a good time.
3. Brenda moved to town in March.
4. The whole family planned a party for Mrs. Williams.
5. They all helped.

Activity C. Write these sentences on your paper. Underline the complete subject. Circle the simple subject.

1. Our neighbor painted his house.
2. His whole family picked out the color.
3. The color was brown.
4. They needed a ladder.
5. The part under the roof was hard to reach.
6. The whole job took them three days.

Activity D. Write the predicate of the sentence on your paper. Underline the simple verb with all of its helping verbs.
Example: We rented a house.   <u>rented</u> a house

1. A popular band was coming to town.
2. Bruce bought two tickets.
3. The concert was on Saturday evening.
4. He decided to take Brenda.
5. Brenda enjoyed music very much.
6. She could feel the vibrations of the band.

- A sentence can have more than one subject or predicate. They are connected with conjunctions. We call them compound subjects or compound predicates.

Compound subject: **Bruce and Brenda** went to the concert.
Compound predicate: The band **sang and played**.

Activity E.   Write the compound subjects or compound predicates on your paper.

1. Bruce went to the auditorium and got the tickets.
2. Brenda and Bruce enjoyed the concert.
3. The band played their instruments and sang.
4. Both the band and the audience had a good time.

There are three kinds of sentences: the *simple sentence*, the *compound sentence*, and the *complex sentence*.

- A *simple sentence* has one subject and one predicate. The subject may be compound. The predicate may be compound.
Examples:
      Bruce and Brenda enjoyed the music.
      The band played well.

- A *compound sentence* has two independent clauses joined together with a coordinating conjunction. A compound sentence could be written as two separate sentences.
Examples:
      <u>They left early</u>, and <u>they got home late</u>.
      Independent Clause   Independent Clause

- A *complex sentence* has an independent clause and a dependent clause. An independent clause can stand alone. It is a complete idea and has a subject and a verb. A dependent clause "depends" on another part of the sentence. It cannot stand alone. Dependent clauses begin with subordinating conjunctions (see chapter 8).

<u>They went home</u> <u>after the concert was over</u>.
Independent Clause   Dependent Clause

Activity F.   Read each of these sentences. Decide whether it is simple, compound, or complex sentence. Write your answers on your paper.

1. I would like a hamburger.
2. The hamburger looks good, but I want barbecue sauce on it.
3. I can't give you barbecue sauce because we are all out of it.
4. I will have the hamburger without the sauce, but it won't taste as good.
5. I will be going to the beach when I am finished eating.

Every sentence has a purpose. Sentences can make statements. They can ask questions. They can give commands or requests.

Statement:	They went to the concert.
Question:	Did they go to the concert?
Command:	Go to the concert.
Request:	Please go to the concert.

Any sentence can express strong feelings. It ends with an exclamation point to show those feelings.

Statement: The concert was great!
Question: Did you see that car!
Command: Stop making that noise!

A sentence that makes a statement usually begins with the subject.

The **concert** began at eight o'clock.

A sentence that asks a question begins with either a helping verb or an interrogative pronoun or adverb.

Examples:

Where are my shoes?   **Are** you ready yet?
Who is she?   **Did** you like the music?

A sentence that makes a command or request begins with a verb. The subject is understood to be the person we are talking to.

(You) **Give** me two tickets.
(You) **Take** your medicine.
(You) **Fill** out this form.

Activity G.   Read these sentences. What is the purpose of each one? Decide whether each is a statement, question, or command.

1. Are you hungry?
2. Yes, I am.
3. Please order something.
4. I would like a milkshake.
5. What kind do you want?
6. I want a chocolate milkshake.
7. Wait just a second.
8. Here is your milkshake.
9. How much is it?
10. Look at the check.

CHAPTER 10

The Subject and the Predicate

Every sentence has two parts. They are the *subject* and the *predicate*. The subject is what we are talking about. The predicate tells us what the subject did or what happened to the subject.

Warm-Up A. Find the subject in each sentence. List these subjects with their modifiers on your paper.

Examples: In the morning **Mary** ate breakfast. — Mary
              Stop it! — *You* is understood as the subject.
              Does **your brother** like tennis? — your brother

1. Mary wanted a cassette player.
2. Her birthday was coming up soon.
3. On Saturday she looked at them in the store.
4. Her mother asked Mary a question.
5. "Would you like anything special for your birthday?"
6. "Please give me a cassette player."
7. April third is Mary's birthday.

The predicate part of a sentence includes the verb. All of the words tell something about the verb. All of the words that are not part of the subject are part of the predicate.

Warm-Up B. Write these sentences. Underline the predicate part of each sentence.
Examples:

<u>Do</u> you <u>like music</u>?
An apple <u>is a good dessert</u>.

1. Many people know about their "sun sign."
2. Astrologers write daily horoscopes for the newspaper.
3. Joanna is an Aries.
4. Harry Houdini, the magician, was also born under that sign.
5. The sign of Aries is a ram.
6. An Aries girl likes to be independent.
7. She will probably open her own doors!

A sentence can contain more than one subject or predicate. In this case, the subject and predicate are called compound. A sentence can also be compound. In this case, the sentence contains two complete ideas.

Warm-Up C. Each sentence below contains a conjunction. Tell whether each sentence has a compound subject, a compound predicate, or whether it is a compound sentence.

1. Thomas Jefferson and Vincent Van Gogh were both Aries.
2. Joanna is an Aries, but Denise is a Gemini.
3. Gemini begins on May 22 and ends on June 21.

Lesson 1. The Subject of the Sentence

The subject is the part of the sentence that tells what is being talked about. The main word in a subject is usually a noun or pronoun.

- The *complete subject* may be one word or many words.

  The French teacher gave the class homework.
  She announced a quiz for Friday.
  The man who taught us French last year moved to another town.

- The *simple subject* is the noun or pronoun.

  The **quiz** on Friday was easy.
  We had to know five French verbs.
  One **girl** in the class had a perfect paper.

- The *complete subject* is usually made up of a noun or pronoun and all of the words that describe it.

  Some popular French songs were sung.

Activity A.   Write the complete subject of each of these sentences on your paper. Circle the simple subject. A complete subject may be only one word.

1. Madame Donet teaches French.
2. The entire class speaks in French every day.
3. The teacher asks the students questions.
4. They must answer in French.
5. The students in the class must work hard.

- The simple subject cannot be the object of the preposition. The prepositional phrase that describes the pronoun is part of the complete subject. The simple subject is in boldface. Examples:

One of the girls was late.

Girls is the object of the preposition *of*; therefore, it cannot be the subject.

Each of the students needs a book.

Students is the object of the preposition *of*; therefore, it cannot be the subject.

Activity B. Find the simple subjects in these sentences. Write each one on your paper.

1. Each of the students wrote the answer on his paper.
2. All of my friends like music.
3. Yesterday eight of the students were absent.
4. All of them had the flu.
5. Two of the students had a fever.

Activity C. Find the complete subject in the following sentences. Write each on your own paper.

1. I am going to the store.
2. Kim and Stephanie are in the same class.
3. Three of our classmates went on the trip.
4. One of my friends lives near me.
5. Everyone in the band is going.

- The subject of a sentence usually comes before the verb, but it may come after the verb. When a sentence begins with *Here* or *There*, the subject comes after the verb.
  Examples:

  > There will be **a bus** at eleven-thirty.
  > Here is **your book**.

Activity D. Find the simple subjects in these sentences. Write each one on your own paper.

1. There is a good program on TV tonight.
2. Here is the bus stop.
3. Here is the correct answer.
4. There is my school.
5. There are no more books about James Polk left in the library.

- In a question, the helping verb or part of the verb phrase may come before the subject.

  >   v   v
  > When does **Mary** have French?

  >   v   v
  > Are **you** leaving soon?

- The interrogative pronoun may be the subject of a sentence that asks a question. The subject in each sentence below is in boldface.

  > **Who** is she?
  > **What** is happening?

- In a command or a request, the subject is *you*, even though the word *you* does not appear in the sentence. The subject is "understood" to be the person we are speaking to.
  Examples:

  > Please fix lunch soon.
  > (**You**) Please fix lunch soon.

  > Jack, stop bothering me.
  > Jack, (**you**) stop bothering me.

- The subject of a sentence can be compound (two subjects).
  Examples:

  > **Mary and Brenda** went to class.
  > **The girl and her friend** went shopping.

Activity E.   Find the simple subject in each of these sentences.

1. Where will the meeting be?
2. What time will the meeting be?
3. What is happening at the meeting?
4. Will you be going to the meeting?
5. Has this group ever met before?

Activity F.   Find the simple subject in each of these sentences.

1. Bruce read the newspaper.
2. Read the newspaper.
3. Bruce, read the newspaper.
4. Read the newspaper, Bruce.
5. Please hurry!

Activity G.   Find the simple subjects in these sentences. Write them on your own paper.

1. Neither Fred nor Tricia went to the concert.
2. Both my hat and my gloves were lost.
3. Spring and summer are my favorite seasons.
4. Please bring my books to class.
5. Are my books or my papers in your locker?
6. There are not enough sodas and snacks for everyone.

Lesson Review

Lesson Review.   Write each of these sentences on your paper. Underline the complete subject. Then circle the simple subject.

1. Soon baseball season begins.
2. Will James be on the team?
3. He usually plays first base.
4. There will be a try-out on Friday.
5. Bruce and Andy like to play baseball.
6. The college has a good team.
7. Most of last year's team graduated.
8. Where will the try-outs be?

Lesson 2. The Predicate

The *complete predicate* of a sentence tells something about the subject. It always has a verb.

> James **helped his father in the garage.**
> Andy **looks at new cars every weekend.**

- The main word in the predicate is the verb or verb phrase. The predicate also includes all of the words that tell something about the verb.
  Examples:
  > James ***helped* his father in the garage.**
  > Andy ***looks* at new cars every weekend.**

Activity A.   Read these sentences. Write only the predicate part of each sentence on your paper.

1. Brenda's earring was lost yesterday.
2. She looked everywhere for it.
3. Denise found it today.
4. One of the stones was missing.
5. Someone apparently stepped on it.
6. Brenda walked home with Denise.
7. Her dog greeted them with loud barks.
8. He tried to cheer up Brenda.
9. The earrings had been her favorite jewelry.

Activity B. Write the predicate of each sentence on your paper. Circle the verb or verb phrase.

1. Mrs. Barry gave Mary a surprise birthday party.
2. Mary's brother Bruce baked the cake.
3. Mr. Barry drove Mary to band practice that day.
4. Her friends came over and decorated the house.
5. Mary came home about six-thirty.
6. They all jumped out.
7. They screamed, "Surprise!"
8. The cake was delicious.
9. Everyone ate two pieces.
10. Bruce was very pleased about that.

- Any word that is not in the subject is in the predicate. Usually the predicate part of the sentence comes after the subject.
  Example:
  > The whole family **enjoyed the party**.

- In a question, part of the predicate often comes before the subject.
  Examples:
  > **Did** you **bring Mary a present**?
  > **Where did** you **put it**?
  > **Was** it **expensive**?

- Adverbs and prepositional phrases that are used as adverbs may be at the beginning of the sentence.
  Examples:
  > **At eleven o'clock** everyone **went home**.
  > **Then** Bruce **ate the last piece of cake**.

Activity C.   Write only the predicate part of each of these sentences on your paper. Circle the verb or verb phrase.

1. Did Denise bring Sheba to the party?
2. Why was Sheba left at home?
3. Maybe she didn't have a present.
4. After the party Denise wrapped up a piece of cake to take home.
5. Was it for Sheba?
6. Sheba is only a cat.
7. She can't really expect a piece of cake.
8. At eleven-thirty Sheba heard Denise's key in the door.
9. Usually she meows happily.
10. Tonight she was unusually quiet.
11. Then she saw the cake in Denise's hand.
12. In an instant, that silly cat was meowing happily.

- The predicate part of the sentence can be compound. A compound predicate has two verbs or verb phrases.
  Examples:
    The sun **moved behind the cloud and disappeared**.
    The audience **clapped and cheered**.

- Remember that an infinitive (*to* + a verb) is not a part of the main verb or verb phrase. It may be part of the predicate.
  Example:
      verb   infinitive
  Mary **decided to leave early**.
      complete predicate

Activity D. Write the predicate part of each of these sentences. Circle each verb or verb phrase.

1. Andy looked at new cars but didn't buy one.
2. The big cars cost too much and used too much gas.
3. The small cars got good gas mileage but were also expensive.
4. The used cars were often rusty and needed repairs.
5. Andy thought and thought but couldn't make a decision.

Activity E. Write five sentences with compound predicates. Then circle each verb or verb phrase in your sentences.

Activity F. Write only the verb or verb phrase in each of these sentences.

1. Do you like to fish?
2. Anna wanted to know the answer.
3. Where do you like to go on vacation?
4. Brenda's family likes to camp.
5. My puppy only likes to eat or bark.

Lesson Review

Lesson Review. Write each of these sentences on your paper. Underline only the predicate part. Then, circle the main verb or verb phrase.

1. In the spring the weather gets warm.
2. People think about outdoor activities.
3. Some of the neighbors are planting flowers.
4. My neighbor Matthew gets his fishing gear out.
5. I always know the first day of spring.
6. He is out in his yard with his fishing rod.
7. He likes to practice casting.
8. This year Matthew plans to catch a huge fish.
9. He wants to catch the big one.
10. Last year it got away.
11. This year will be different.
12. He has already invited us to the fish fry.

Lesson 3. Compound Sentences

A *simple sentence* is an independent clause. A *compound sentence* has two or more independent clauses joined together with a conjunction. Each clause has a subject and a predicate and expresses a complete idea.

Subject   Predicate   Subject   Predicate
<u>Bruce</u> <u>took his car to the garage</u>, and <u>the mechanic</u> <u>changed the oil</u>.

- A compound sentence tells about two or more related events.

    Correct: The mechanic fixed the car, and Bruce drove it home.

    Incorrect: The mechanic changed the oil, and gas costs a lot these days.

Activity A.   Write these sentences on your paper. Underline each subject once and each predicate twice.

1. After the party they were hungry; however, all of the restaurants were closed.
2. Alice has a cat, Mike has a gerbil, and Sandy has a hamster.
3. Mr. Barry likes sweets, but Mrs. Barry prefers fruit.
4. Andy wants to be a catcher, but Bruce likes to play third base.
5. The new French teacher gives a lot of homework, but his tests are usually easy.

Activity B.   Write five compound sentences. Be sure the ideas are related. Punctuate them correctly.

- Remember that a simple sentence may have a compound subject or a compound predicate. A compound sentence must have two or more complete ideas.

Activity C.   Number your paper from 1 to 5. Read these sentences. After each number write *Yes* if the sentence is compound. Write *No* if it is not a compound sentence.

1. Toyotas and Chevettes are small cars.
2. Andy is always looking at cars, but he hasn't bought one yet.
3. The telephone rang three times and then stopped.
4. The girls hurried, but they were late anyway.
5. After school we came home, ate dinner, did homework, and went to bed.

Lesson Review

Lesson Review.   Write each of these sentences on your paper. Underline the subject once and the predicate twice. Then decide whether or not the sentence is compound.

1. Andy counted his money and made a decision.
2. Most of the cars in town were too expensive, but one form of transportation was just right.
3. He needed something to drive to work, and he also needed something to drive to school.
4. Bruce and Andy went to the showroom.
5. Andy's new "wheels" were there, and they looked great.
6. The motorcycle was not a fancy car, but Andy was happy!

CHAPTER REVIEW

Part A.   Write each sentence on your paper. Underline the subject once and the predicate twice.

1. Everyone liked Andy's new motorcycle.
2. Denise and Mary wanted a ride.
3. Andy gave Denise a crash helmet.
4. She hopped on the back and smiled.
5. "Have you ever ridden on a bike before?"
6. She shook her head.
7. "Then this ride will be especially fun."
8. There was a small breeze that day.
9. They rode around the block and returned.
10. "Give me a turn!"

Part B. Write each sentence on your paper. Underline the subject once and the predicate twice. Then decide whether or not the sentence is compound.

1. The motorcycle took off, and Corey screamed.
2. "It is going too fast for me!"
3. Corey held on tightly, but he was still afraid.
4. Denise and Bruce stood on the curb and waited for Andy and Corey.
5. In a few minutes Andy pulled up, and Corey got off.
6. "That was fun, but I prefer a car."
7. Corey bent down and kissed the ground.
8. Bruce just shook his head.

CHAPTER 11

Sentence Patterns

There are only a few basic sentence patterns in the English language. In this chapter you will study four of those patterns.

Pattern 1. Pattern 1 has an intransitive verb. Sometimes an adverb or prepositional phrase is added to express a complete idea. A pattern 1 sentence tells *who did*.
Example:

       S   I.V.
     She laughed.

Pattern 2. Pattern 2 has a transitive verb and a direct object. You may also add adverbs and prepositional phrases. A pattern 2 sentence tells *who did what*.
Example:

      S   T.V.   D.O.
    Alison has a trumpet.

Pattern 3.   Pattern 3 has a transitive verb and a direct object. It also has an indirect object. A pattern 3 sentence tells *who did what to whom* (or *for whom*).
Example:

> S   T.V.   I.O.   D.O.
> She gave me a book.

Pattern 4.   Pattern 4 has a transitive verb. It has a direct object. It also has an objective complement. The objective complement renames or describes the object.
Example:

> S   T.V.   D.O.   O.C.
> We painted the house red.

Warm-Up.   Look at the examples above. Try to identify the pattern of each of these sentences.

1. We gave John a new record.
2. The Rolling Stones made that record.
3. They made the record cover silver.
4. John listened to the record.
5. The book is on the shelf.
6. The band raised money for the trip.
7. Alison fixed everyone dinner.
8. We elected John president.

Lesson 1. Pattern 1 Sentences

Pattern 1 sentences are the simplest kind of sentence pattern. You need only a subject and a verb to express a complete thought. The verb in these sentences is intransitive. An intransitive verb does not have an object. The action is not done to anyone or anything. Helping verbs may be included.

Pattern 1 Sentence: Subject + Verb

Sue smiled.
The sun **was shining**.

Activity A.   Write each of these sentences on your paper. Draw a line between the subject and the verb.
Example:
The dog / was barking.

1. The band was playing.
2. The audience clapped.
3. Donna laughed.
4. The kitten purred.
5. She has been practicing.
6. They were singing.
7. I am listening.
8. My best friend moved.
9. The people on the next block are painting.
10. Dinner is burning!

- You can add an adverb to Pattern 1 sentences. The adverb answers a question about the verb. An adverb tells, *Where*, *How*, or *When*. The adverb may come between the helping verb and the main verb.

  Examples:

  The kitten purred **softly**.
  The dog barked **loudly**.
  John is **often** late.

Activity B. Make two columns on your paper. In the first column, write the verb or verb phrase from each sentence. In the second column, write the adverb.

1. The fire is burning brightly.
2. Victor can run fast.
3. Sara is usually smiling.
4. Alison practices often.
5. I am reading now.
6. Nora is walking rapidly.
7. Yesterday it rained.

Activity C. Use each of these verbs in a sentence. Underline the subject once and the predicate twice.

1. go
2. walk
3. work
4. fall
5. live
6. laugh
7. scream
8. cry
9. inquire
10. think

- A prepositional phrase may be added to the Pattern 1 sentence. The prepositional phrase may act like an adjective and describe the subject. It may act like an adverb and tell about the verb. Example:

  Sue is walking **to the store**.

Sue is not doing anything *to* the store. The phrase, *to the store*, tells us where she is walking.

Activity D. Write each sentence on your paper. Circle the verb. Then underline the prepositional phrase that tells about the action.

1. Everyone laughs at the clown.
2. Karl is leaving for school.
3. Our neighbors moved to Ohio.
4. Mr. Nelson works at the post office.
5. The book fell off the shelf.

A Pattern 1 sentence:
- a. must have a subject and a verb.
- b. may have an adverb.
- c. may have a prepositional phrase.

Activity E. Write ten Pattern 1 sentences on your paper. Your sentences may have an adverb or a prepositional phrase. The subject may not be doing anything to another person or another thing.

A Pattern 1 sentence may be a question. Part of the verb may be used to form the question. You may need to add a helping verb.

Statement: The cat **is scratching**.
Question: **Is** the cat **scratching**?

Statement: Kristen **walked** on the beach.
Question: **Did** Kristen **walk** on the beach?

Activity F.   Read these sentences. Find the verbs and verb phrases. List each one on your paper.

1. Will Karl leave soon?
2. Which book fell off the shelf?
3. Where does Mr. Nelson work?
4. Is Alison still practicing?
5. Are you listening to the radio?

Activity G.   Here are ten sentences. See if you can recognize a Pattern 1 sentence. Five of them follow Pattern 1. Number your paper from 1 to 10. Write *Yes* after the number if the sentence follows Pattern 1. Write *No* if it does not follow Pattern 1.

1. Alison's band is going to Florida.
2. The band will play for a large audience.
3. The band entered a contest.
4. Everyone has been practicing for weeks.
5. The band members are saving money.
6. They will go on a bus.
7. They will stay in a hotel in Miami.
8. Mrs. Nelson told Alison to send her a postcard.
9. Tim wants a T-shirt.
10. Rita bought a flute!

- A Pattern 1 sentence may have a compound subject.
  Example:
  Sue and Rita will leave soon.

- A Pattern 1 sentence may have a compound predicate.
  Example:
  The band **will go to Florida and play**.

- Two Pattern 1 sentences may be joined with a conjunction.
  Together, they will form a compound sentence.
  Example:
  Mrs. Nelson laughed at the joke, **but** Mr. Nelson only smiled.

Activity H. Write the sentences below on your paper. Then do the
following exercises:
  A. Find the complete subject or subjects. Underline them once.
  B. Then, circle the simple subjects.
  C. Next, find the complete predicate, or predicates.
     Underline them twice.
  D. Then, circle the verbs or verb phrases.

These sentences will have a compound subject or a compound
predicate. They may also be compound sentences.

1. The book and the pencil fell on the floor.
2. Alison laughed first and then cried.
3. Alison and the band are thinking about their trip and talking to
   each other.
4. Alison and Frank were on time, but they had to run down the hall.
5. Clarissa was reading in the morning, and she was writing in the
   afternoon.

Activity I.   Expand these Pattern 1 sentences by adding adverbs and prepositional phrases to the predicate.   (Add only adverbs or prepositional phrases.)
Examples:

> The girl walked.
> The girl walked **quickly to the store**.

1. The dog barked.
2. The fire burned.
3. The boys left.
4. Tricia listened.
5. The lady laughed.
6. The man ate.
7. Snow fell.
8. We talked.
9. Bob is running.
10. His sister works.

Activity J.   Write these sentences on your paper.   Underline the basic sentence.
Example:

> The teacher listened closely to the students.
> The teacher listened.

1. The band played loudly at the dance.
2. Mrs. Nelson left in a hurry.
3. Everyone laughed loudly at the joke.
4. Which student reported during first period?
5. Is my dog barking at the cat now?
6. Several of the people cried during the movie.
7. Emilio's motorcycle rides smoothly.
8. He inquired about the guarantee.
9. Are you leaving for school now?
10. Alison's band will go to Florida and play in a contest.

Diagraming Pattern 1 Sentences

- A sentence diagram is a picture of a sentence that helps you see the parts of the sentence more clearly. Study the rules for diagraming Pattern 1 sentences.

Rule 1:   Draw a horizontal line under the entire sentence.
Divide it into two parts with a short vertical line.

Rule 2:   The word on the left is the simple subject (a noun or pronoun).
The word on the right is the simple predicate (a verb or verb phrase).
Example: Sue smiled.

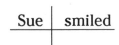

Rule 3:   Adjectives or prepositional phrases that describe the subject go under the subject.

Rule 4:   Adverbs or prepositional phrases that tell about the verb go under the verb.
Example: The small kitten beside me purred softly.

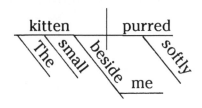

Activity K.   Diagram the five sentences below. Follow the rules for diagraming Pattern 1 sentences.

1. The school band went on a trip.
2. Alison went, too.
3. They went on a bus.
4. The band left in May.
5. The trip lasted for one week.

Lesson Review

Lesson Review.   Write each of these sentences on your paper. Underline the complete subject once and the complete predicate twice.

1. Which students are in the band room?
2. Everyone will ride on the bus.
3. Alison's trumpet fell on the floor.
4. Luckily, it did not break.
5. Alison almost cried!
6. Alison is ready for the trip.
7. Everyone in the band is thinking about the trip.
8. Sue and Rita are not going.
9. They will stay in school.
10. The band has been practicing and preparing for the trip for a long time.

Lesson 2. Pattern 2 Sentences

A Pattern 2 sentence contains a transitive verb. A transitive verb has an object. The action is transferred to another person or thing. The object of the verb is a noun or pronoun.

Pattern 2 Sentence: Subject + Verb + Direct Object
                                S   V   D.O.
                        Mrs. Nelson bought a new hat.
                                S   V   D.O.
                        She has new shoes too.

Activity A.   The verb in each of these sentences is in boldface. Find the object and write it on your paper.

1. Len **found** the verbs.
2. He **wrote** them on his paper.
3. Then Len **located** the objects.
4. He **listed** them in order.
5. Len **raised** his hand.
6. I **have found** the answers to these questions.

Activity B.   Write each of these sentences on your paper. Add a noun or pronoun that completes the thought.

1. Howard bought _____ .
2. We saw _____ .
3. For dinner we fixed _____ .
4. I bought _____ yesterday.
5. Have you ever studied _____ ?
6. My kitten lost _____ .

• You know that the subject of a sentence is usually a noun or pronoun. The object of the verb is also a noun or pronoun.

Noun Used as a Subject: **Janine** baked a cake.
Noun Used as an Object: I saw **Janine**.

Pronoun Used as a Subject: **She** baked a cake.
Pronoun Used as an Object: Tracy saw **her**.

FORMS OF PERSONAL PRONOUNS

Singular	Subject	Object
First person	I	me
Second person	you	you
Third person	he	him
	she	her
	it	it
Plural		
First person	we	us
Second person	you	you
Third person	they	them

Activity C. Write these sentences. Add the correct form of the pronoun in each sentence.

1. _____ wrote a letter. (I, me)
2. Did you see _____ ? (he, him)
3. Fred found _____ in the library. (he, him)
4. Bill finally found _____ . (they, them)
5. _____ bought some new shoes. (She, Her)
6. _____ really liked that movie. (We, Us)

Activity D. Across your paper write three headings: Subject, Verb, Object. Write the parts of the sentences below in the correct columns. Example:

Subject	**Verb**	**Object**
My Aunt Anita	bought	a condominium.
She	fixed	her bicycle.

1. Sam received a letter.
2. The tabby cat caught a mouse.
3. I have been studying French.
4. The firefighters were climbing the ladders.
5. Mr. Nelson loves that old song!
6. We cannot find her.

• The predicate of the Pattern 2 sentence must have a verb and an object. It may also have an adverb.

Adverb   V   D.O.
<u>Luckily</u> Alison <u>found</u> <u>her trumpet</u>.

              V   D.O.   Adverb
Emilio <u>bought</u> <u>a motorcycle</u> <u>yesterday</u>.

Adverb V D.O.
I <u>just</u> <u>found</u> <u>it</u>.

Activity E. Write the complete predicate of each of these sentences on your paper. (HINT: Find the complete subject first. All of the words left over are in the predicate.)

1. Tim bought his tickets early.
2. You can diagram this sentence.
3. Kevin eats his dinner rapidly.
4. You can easily find the subject.
5. Yesterday Dan lost his notebook.
6. He found it today.

- The predicate part of a Pattern 2 sentence may also have a prepositional phrase.

V   D.O.   Prepositional Phrase

Alison <u>found</u> <u>her trumpet</u> <u>in the band room</u>.

- The object of the verb is a noun. You may add adjectives and prepositional phrases that describe the object.

V   Adjective   D.O. Prepositional Phrase

We <u>baked</u> <u>a chocolate</u> <u>cake</u> <u>with vanilla icing</u>.

Activity F. Write only the predicate part of each sentence. Then underline the verb and its object. Draw a circle around the prepositional phrase.

1. Alison wrote a letter to her uncle Albert.
2. My neighbors painted their house with bright colors.
3. My dog wanted a new food dish for his birthday.
4. We filled the fish tank to the top.
5. Tim made pancakes for breakfast.
6. Sara found some blue shoes with white trim.

Activity G. Write some Pattern 2 sentences using the verbs below. Each sentence must have a subject, a verb, and an object. You may also add adverbs and prepositional phrases.

1. break
2. bring
3. buy
4. catch
5. choose
6. dig
7. freeze
8. have
9. spend
10. take

- Pattern 2 sentences may be questions. Remember that part of the verb is often placed before the subject to form a question.

                   V   D.O.

  Statement: I <u>saw</u> <u>a deer</u> cross the road.

                   V   V   D.O.

  Question: <u>Did</u> I <u>see</u> <u>a deer</u> cross the road?

- Pattern 2 sentences may also be commands or requests. Remember that the subject of a command or request is always understood to be *you*. The word *you* may or may not appear.

          V   D.O.

  Type my letter!

             V   D.O.

  Then mail it, please.

Activity H. Find the verb or verb phrase and the object in each sentence. Write them on your paper.

1. The secretary typed a letter.
2. Is the secretary typing your letter?
3. Have you finished my letter yet?
4. Who is typing my letter?
5. Can you type my letter?
6. Has anyone seen my letter?

Activity I. Write each sentence on your paper. Circle the verb or verb phrase. Underline the object.

1. Take this book to the library.
2. Make a chocolate cake for dessert, please.
3. Finish your work at home.
4. Hang your coat in the closet.
5. Have another piece of chocolate cake!
6. Read these sentences carefully!

- A Pattern 2 sentence may have compound parts. You may join two Pattern 2 sentences together with a conjunction.

Compound Verb: We **baked** the cake and **frosted** it.

Compound Object: We baked **a pie** and **a cake**.

Compound Sentence: **I found Paul**, but **he didn't have my books**.

Activity J.   Expand these Pattern 2 sentences by adding adverbs, adjectives, and prepositional phrases.

Example:
> We baked a cake.
> We baked a **chocolate** cake **in home economics class**.

1. Have you read that book?
2. Karl doesn't like that song.
3. Everyone enjoyed the party.
4. Wanda found Sharon in the lunchroom.
5. Carol can speak French.
6. Fix this car.
7. Please do your work.
8. Bring a main dish and a dessert.
9. Sue and Rita bought shoes.
10. Tim has a part-time job; however, he also takes classes at the community college.

Diagraming Pattern 2 Sentences

Rule 1:   In a diagram, the object is placed on the base line. A short vertical line separates the verb and the object.

We baked cookies.

| We | baked | cookies |

Rule 2:   Put each adverb, adjective, or prepositional phrase under the word it is describing or telling about.

That man bought the last ticket to the show.

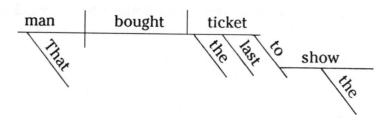

Rule 3:   The understood subject of a command or a request is shown in parentheses.

Fix my car quickly.

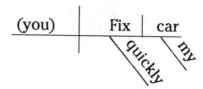

Rule 4:   If the sentence is a question, change it into a statement. Then draw the diagram.

Did you find your coat?
You did find your coat.

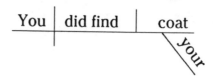

Activity K.   Diagram these sentences. Look at the examples on pages 229-230.

1. Please stop that noise!
2. Jack left his book in his locker.
3. Have you seen Sally?
4. Rita likes poetry by Edgar Allan Poe.
5. Mrs. Nelson has blue eyes.
6. We bought a ticket for the early show.
7. He fixed the car quickly.

Lesson Review

Part A.   Find the direct object of the verb in each of these sentences. List these words on your own paper.

1. Evan asked several questions.
2. The teacher answered the questions.
3. Laura knows Sue very well.
4. Sue knows Rita and Alison, too.
5. Have you seen that movie?
6. No, but I read the book.
7. Did you like it?
8. Yes, it had a good story.

Part B.   Read these sentences. Decide whether they follow Pattern 1 (intransitive verb) or Pattern 2 (transitive verb). Write your answers.

1. We met at three o'clock.
2. Alison met Rita at three o'clock.
3. Will the band win the contest?
4. When are they leaving for Florida?
5. Please pack your suitcase tonight.
6. The bus leaves at five tomorrow morning.

Lesson 3. Pattern 3 Sentences

A Pattern 3 sentence has a transitive verb, a direct object, and an indirect object. The indirect object tells who will receive the direct object. An indirect object is a noun or pronoun that names the person receiving the direct object.

Pattern 3 Sentence:

Subject + Verb + Indirect Object + Direct Object

        S   V   I.O.   D.O.
Mrs. Nelson gave Alison a dollar.

Mrs. Nelson gave the **dollar**.
(*Dollar* is the direct object.)

Alison received the dollar.
(*Alison* is the indirect object.)

Important!   A sentence cannot have an indirect object unless it has a direct object.

Important!   The indirect object comes before the direct object in a sentence.

Activity A.   Read these sentences. Find the indirect objects and list them on your paper.

1. Rita gave her mother a gift.
2. They gave Alison the prize.
3. The team awarded Jim the prize.
4. We asked her a question.
5. Rita told Sue the answer.
6. Mr. Harris taught Tim math.
7. The bank lent Mr. Nelson some money.
8. The salesclerk handed Alison the bill.
9. Emilio allows himself a dollar for lunch.
10. Emilio offered Tim his dessert.

- You may find the indirect object by rewriting the sentence. You may make the indirect object into a prepositional phrase by adding the words *to* or *for.*
  Example: I.O.   D.O.
              Emilio offered Tim his dessert.
                              D.O.   Prep. Phrase
              Emilio offered his dessert to Tim.

Activity B.   Rewrite each of these sentences. Change the indirect object to a prepositional phrase.
Example: I bought Mary a gift. I bought a gift **for Mary**.

1. Rita gave her dog a bone.
2. Mrs. Nelson paid the grocer twenty dollars.
3. Emilio lent Tim his motorcycle.
4. Sue asked Alison a question.
5. The waitress served Sue and Alison lunch.
6. Mother bought Tim a gift.

Activity C. Rewrite each of these sentences. Change the prepositional phrase to an indirect object.
Example:
> The postman handed **her mail to Mrs. Nelson.**
> The postman handed **Mrs. Nelson her mail**.

1. The teacher found a book for Alison.
2. Tim bought a new coat for himself.
3. Sue handed the note to Rita.
4. Alison fixed lunch for herself.
5. The university gave a diploma to the student.

Activity D. On your paper, draw a chart with four columns. Title the columns: Subject, Verb, Indirect Object, Direct Object. List the parts of these sentences in the correct columns.
Example:

Subject	Verb	Indirect Object	Direct Object
Mary	gave	me	a present.

1. The director gave the band members their music.
2. Fred asked Mr. Smith a question.
3. The music company sent the school a bill.
4. Mr. Smith handed Alison her trumpet.
5. Mr. Smith offered the students his help.
6. The teacher gave the class homework.
7. Sue taught Rita sign language.
8. Alison wrote her aunt a letter.
9. The school awarded Tim a scholarship.
10. Mr. Jackson gave Tim a raise.

Activity E.   Rearrange the words in each line to make a Pattern 3 sentence.

1. me told Sue secret a
2. made Tim cake Alison a
3. them served waitress dinner the
4. her a letter wrote Rita aunt
5. gave rose Erica Emilio a
6. told team the coach play the the
7. a ribbon Tracy Rita bought
8. herself snack fixed Alison a
9. me her sweater Alison lent
10. a him he handed dollar

• When the indirect object is a pronoun, it must be in the objective case. Refer to the chart on page 224.

Activity F.   Write each of these sentences on your paper. Fill in the correct form of the pronoun in the space.

1. ____ gave Tom a message. (I , me)
2. Fred sent ____ a letter. (he, him)
3. Martha told ____ the answer. (she, her)
4. That teacher taught ____ French. (we, us)
5. ____ offered the lady our seats. (We, Us)
6. We served ____ dinner. (they, them)

- To Pattern 3 sentences, you may add adjectives which describe the indirect object. You may also add prepositional phrases.
  Examples:
  Sentence: I wrote my sister a letter.
  Adjective: I wrote my **younger** sister a letter.

  Sentence: She gave her friend a gift.
  Prepositional Phrase: She gave her friend **from Montana** a gift.

Activity G.   Read these sentences. The indirect object is in boldface. Write each sentence on your paper. Add an adjective or prepositional phrase that describes the indirect object.

1. Pat gave her **friend** a message.
2. Rita offered the **lady** her seat.
3. The teacher told the **boy** the answer.
4. We made our **neighbor** an offer.
5. The newspaper boy brought the **people** their newspaper.

- Pattern 3 sentences can be questions. Part of the verb phrase may be placed before the subject. The question may also begin with an interrogative word.
  Examples:

  I.O.
  Will you **give** Shawn a message?
  I.O.
  Who made me this chocolate cake?

- Pattern 3 sentences are often commands or requests.
  Examples:

  > Please send your uncle a letter.
  > Give me his new address.

Activity H.   Find the indirect objects in these sentences. List them on your own paper.

1. Rita, did you give your cat his dinner?
2. Would you lend me your sweater for the evening?
3. Who asked Alison that question?
4. When did the teacher find Alison a book?
5. In what year did Christopher Columbus discover America?

Activity I.   Find the indirect objects in these sentences. List them on your own paper.

1. Tell me the answer.
2. Please teach me Spanish.
3. Mom, bake us a cake for dessert tonight.
4. Tell me the truth.
5. Allow yourself enough time for breakfast.

- The indirect object can be compound.
  Example:

  > Indirect Object
  > Fix your **father and his friend** some coffee.
  > Indirect Object
  > Will you give **Tim and Emilio** a message?

Activity J. Write each of these sentences on your paper. Add a compound indirect object in the space.

1. Write _____ a letter.
2. Give _____ more time.
3. Please tell _____ the answer.
4. Uncle Fred made _____ model airplanes.
5. Would you lend _____ five dollars?

• A Pattern 2 sentence has a direct object. A Pattern 3 sentence has an indirect object and a direct object.

Activity K. In the following sentences, decide which are Pattern 3 sentences and which are Pattern 2 sentences. Write the correct answers on your paper.

1. Have you read that book?
2. Will you read me the book?
3. Read the book to me.
4. Bring your records to the party.
5. Would you bring me a book from the library?
6. Tim drove Emilio to school yesterday.
7. Could you drive me to school today?
8. Victor made his mother a lamp at school.
9. He also made a sewing box.
10. Who made you that lovely sewing box?

Diagraming Pattern 3 Sentences

In a diagram, the indirect object looks like a prepositional phrase. The line where the preposition would go is left blank. Put it under the verb.

Jack gave him a pencil.

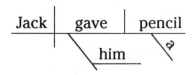

Here are examples of sentences with compounds.

Compound Subject: Alison and Sue laughed.

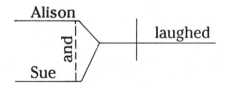

Compound Verb: They ran and ran.

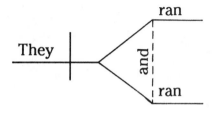

Compound Direct Object: Dan brought Ann and Meg.

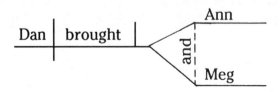

Compound Indirect Object: Give Tim and me a ride.

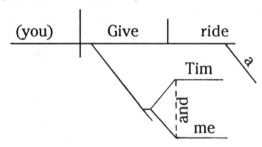

Activity L.   Diagram these Pattern 3 sentences. Look at the examples on page 239.

1. Please pass me the bread.
2. Jack lent Larry his car.
3. Jane made Yolanda an offer for her bike.
4. Lana wrote her married sister a letter.
5. Will you bring me some ice cream?

Lesson Review

Part A.   Find the indirect objects in these sentences. List them on your own paper.

1. Sue brought Rita and Pam some books.
2. After dinner, Grandpa told the family some old stories.
3. Tim asked his grandfather a question.
4. Will you tell me the story about Dad again?
5. Allow yourself several hours for that report.

Part B.   Read each of these sentences. Decide whether it follows Pattern 1, Pattern 2, or Pattern 3. Write the correct answer on your paper.

1. Alison and Tim like Grandfather's stories.
2. Tell us another one!
3. Grandfather tells very long stories.
4. They last for a long time.
5. Would you please fix me a soda and some ice cream?

Lesson 4. Pattern 4 Sentences

A Pattern 4 sentence has a transitive verb, a direct object, and an objective complement. A *complement* is a word that completes an idea. An *objective complement* is a noun or an adjective that completes the meaning of the direct object.

Pattern 4 Sentence:

Subject + Verb + Direct Object + Objective Complement

S   V   D.O.   Complement

The Smiths named their baby Christopher.

Christopher renames the direct object. It is a noun.

S   V   D.O.   Complement

The neighbors painted their house blue.

Blue describes the direct object. It is an adjective.

- The objective complement comes after the direct object in the sentence. It will be either a noun or an adjective.

Activity A. Find the objective complements in these sentences. List them on your paper.

1. The people elected George Washington president in 1788.
2. The frost turned the leaves many colors.
3. Happiness made the girl beautiful.
4. The police found the man dead.
5. The dark room made us sleepy.
6. Everyone calls Laurence Olivier a great actor.
7. They made Mrs. Schwartz president of the company.
8. Emilio considers Alison beautiful.
9. Are you making the cake sweet?
10. The hot sun turned the grass brown.

242

Activity B.   Add an objective complement to each of these groups of words. You may add either a noun or an adjective. Be sure your sentence makes sense. Write the sentence on your paper.

1. He found science class _____.
2. The artist made the pictures _____ .
3. We elected Karl _____ .
4. Don't make the soup _____ .
5. They called him _____ .

Activity C.   Write Pattern 4 sentences using the verbs below.

1. make or made
2. elect or elected
3. find or found
4. name or named
5. turn or turned

Diagraming Pattern 4 Sentences

In a diagram the objective complement goes on the base line. The objective complement is necessary to express a complete thought. Here is what the diagram looks like.

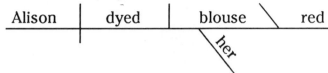

Alison dyed her blouse red.

Important!   The line before the objective complement, *red*, is slanted toward the direct object, *blouse*.

Activity D.   **Diagram** the following sentences.

1. Emilio found his computer class interesting.
2. His classmates elected Jack treasurer.
3. She made the pie spicy.
4. They named Mrs. Nelson "Woman of the Year."
5. Alison painted her room yellow.

Lesson Review

Lesson Review.   Read these sentences.   Find the objective complements. List them on your own paper.

1. They named the young boy the winner.
2. We made Joe our leader.
3. Old age turned her hair silver.
4. They dyed the wool many colors.
5. You made that dinner too fattening!

CHAPTER REVIEW

Part A.   Transitive and Intransitive Verbs

Read each of these sentences. The verb is in boldface. Decide whether the verb is transitive or intransitive.

1. One day Mr. Nelson **bought** a computer.
2. He **called** it a microcomputer.
3. Micro **means** very small.
4. He **attached** the computer to the TV set.
5. The whole family **looked** at the computer.
6. **Can** we **use** it?
7. The computer **could show** video games.
8. Mrs. Nelson **put** her recipe file on the computer.
9. They **used** it for their tax records.
10. That computer **ran** all evening!

Part B.   Sentence Patterns

Read each sentence below. Identify the sentence pattern it follows. Write the pattern number for each sentence.

Pattern 1:   Subject + Verb (adverb)
Pattern 2:   Subject + Verb + Direct Object
Pattern 3:   Subject + Verb + Indirect and Direct Objects
Pattern 4:   Subject + Verb + Direct Object + Objective Complement

1. We can be out math on the microcomputer.
2. It can add fast!
3. Emilio and Tim asked the computer a question.
4. We should give the computer a name!
5. We will call it Einstein!

Part C.   **Diagraming Sentences**

Diagram the following five sentences.

1. We can do our math on the microcomputer.
2. It can add fast!
3. Emilio and Tim asked the computer a question.
4. We should give the computer a name!
5. We will call it Einstein!

CHAPTER 12

Sentence Patterns With a Linking Verb

A *linking verb* is always a state-of-being verb. It does not express action. It is also intransitive. A linking verb cannot have a direct object.

Action verb: James plays baseball.
Linking verb: James is a baseball player.

Warm-Up A. The verb in each of these sentences is in boldface. Decide whether it is an action verb or a linking verb. Write your answer on your own paper.

1. James **has** a new glove.
2. He **bought** the glove from Ted.
3. He **is** a good fielder.
4. James **is** also a good hitter.
5. James **likes** the new glove very much.
6. It **was** expensive.

- A linking verb joins the subject to a word in the predicate part of the sentence.

  Here are the two sentence patterns with linking verbs.
  - Subject — Linking Verb— Adjective
  - Subject — Linking Verb— Noun or Pronoun

Examples:

S L.V. adj.	S L.V. N
Paul is **tall**.	Paul is a **student**.

Warm-Up B. Find the linking verbs in these sentences. List them on your paper.

1. Maryanne's Aunt Pat keeps active.
2. She is sixty years old.
3. Maryanne and Aunt Pat are good friends.
4. Aunt Pat is always happy.
5. She is Mr. Jones' sister.

- A subject and a linking verb do not express a complete thought by themselves. They need an adjective, a noun, or a pronoun to complete the idea.

  Not a sentence: The pudding tastes.
  A complete sentence: The pudding tastes good.

Warm-Up C. Find the adjective, noun, or pronoun that completes the thought in each sentence. List these words on your paper.

1. Sue seems friendly.
2. Sometimes she is shy.
3. She is a good student.
4. Kelly and Maryanne became friends with Sue.
5. Sue is a senior, also.

Lesson 1. Pattern 5 Sentences

A Pattern 5 sentence has a subject, a linking verb, and a predicate adjective.

Pattern 5 Sentences: Subject + Linking Verb + Adjective

| S   L.V.   Adj. | S   L.V.   Adj. |
| The car is expensive. | It looks great! |

- The predicate adjective describes the subject in Pattern 5 sentences. This adjective is needed to complete the thought.

Not a sentence: This book is.
A complete sentence: This book is new.

Activity A.   Add an adjective that will complete each sentence. Write the complete sentence on your paper.

1. Today the air feels _____ .
2. The sky looks _____ .
3. The day is _____ .
4. Everyone feels _____ .
5. They appear _____ .

- The linking verb is needed to help express the complete idea. Imagine that Jeffrey wants to say something about his sister Maryanne.

Tell me about your sister.   Maryanne pretty.

The words, *Maryanne pretty*, do not express a complete thought. Jeffrey needs a word to "link" his subject and the adjective that describes *Maryanne.* He needs a linking verb.

Tell me about Maryanne.   Maryanne **is** pretty.

Activity B.   Add a linking verb to each of these groups of words. Write the sentence on your paper.

1. Lemons sour.
2. The sky blue.
3. Today warm.
4. James athletic.
5. Mrs. Jones serious.
6. The clouds fluffy.
7. Summer hot.
8. Mr. Jones friendly.
9. Maryanne pretty.
10. Sue shy.
11. The air chilly.
12. The motorcycle fun.

An adjective always describes a noun or pronoun.

• Adjectives may appear before nouns.
    My little sister is **a good** student.
    Andy's new car was parked in front of **Maryanne's** house.

• Adjectives may also appear after linking verbs.
    The weather is **sunny** and **mild** today.

• When an adjective appears after a linking verb, it is describing the subject. This adjective is called a *predicate adjective*. It is in the predicate, but it describes the subject of the sentence.

Activity C.   Find all of the adjectives in these sentences. List them on your paper in order. Beside each one, write the noun or pronoun it is describing.
   Example:

My brother is **funny**.
My — brother
funny — brother

1. New cars can be expensive.
2. That little boy looks hungry.
3. My youngest brother grows taller and taller.
4. The birthday cake was chocolate.
5. Tomorrow will be warm and sunny.

- A Pattern 5 sentence has a subject, a linking verb, and an adjective. The adjective is in the predicate, but it describes the subject.

Activity D.   Make three columns on your paper. Title them Subject, Linking Verb, and Adjective. Read the sentences below. Write the parts of each sentence in the three columns.
   Example:
Jim's report was interesting.

Subject	Linking Verb	Adjective
Jim's report	was	interesting.

1. The sunset was lovely.
2. My cousin is artistic.
3. The state of Florida is warm.
4. Rubik's cube is colorful.
5. The apartment is large.

- You may add an adverb of degree to the Pattern 5 sentence. Adverbs of degree answer questions about adjectives.

            S   L.V. Adv. Adj.
        The day was very warm.

- You may also add an adverb or a prepositional phrase to answer questions about the verb.

        She is **always** busy **after school**.
        How often? **always**
        When?   **after school**

Activity E.   Find the predicate adjective in each of these sentences. Then add an adverb of degree.

Example: I feel good today.
              I feel **extremely** good today.

1. My grandmother keeps active.
2. She looks well.
3. She doesn't look old.
4. In fact, my grandmother looks young!
5. Grandma is spry for her age!

Activity F.   Write these sentences on your paper. Add adverbs or prepositional phrases that tell about the verbs.

1. Jim is tall.
2. The cookies are chewy.
3. That house is run-down.
4. The sky looks dark.
5. That painting is colorful.
6. Your salad is delicious.
7. Andy is active.
8. Ted seems quiet.
9. This motor sounds funny.
10. The notebook was neat.

Activity G.   Find the basic sentence pattern in each of these sentences. Write it on your paper.

Example:

The park is usually empty after dark.

S   L.V.   Adj.
The park is empty.

1. The month of June is usually pleasant.
2. The days grow longer then.
3. The air feels warmer in June.
4. Maryanne is especially happy about warm weather.
5. The cat becomes friskier, too.

- The predicate adjective may be compound.
  Example:

$$\begin{array}{ccc} S & L.V. & Adjective \end{array}$$
  Jim's report was **short and funny**.

Activity H. Write these sentences on your paper. Complete them with compound predicate adjectives.

1. The new curtains were ____ and ____ .
2. Maryanne's speech will be ____ or ____ .
3. Andy's motorcycle is ____ but not ____ .
4. The month of May is ____ and ____ .
5. Usually after dinner Mr. Jones is ____ and ____ .

- You may combine two Pattern 5 sentences with a conjunction. You will have a compound sentence.
  Example:

$$\begin{array}{cccccc} S & L.V. & Adj. & S & L.V. & Adj. \end{array}$$
  Mrs. Jones is usually serious, but Mr. Jones is more relaxed.

- A Pattern 5 sentence may be a command or request.
  Example:

  Be quiet!
  Please close the door.

The imperative form of the verb *to be* is always *be*. Remember that commands are always in the present tense.

- A Pattern 5 sentence may also be a question.
  Examples:

  Statement: Jim's report was short.
  Question: Was Jim's report short?

  Statement: April was warm this year.
  Question: Was April warm this year?

Activity I.   Read each of these sentences. Write only the linking verb and the predicate adjective on your paper.

Example:

Keep quiet during my report!
Keep quiet.

1. Look friendly during the job interview.
2. Be nice to your teacher!
3. Be careful on that motorcycle.
4. Be ready for your class.
5. Remain loyal and true to your friends.

Diagraming Pattern 5 Sentences

The predicate adjective is placed on the base line of the diagram. The adjective is necessary to have a complete thought. Because the adjective describes the subject, the line slants toward the subject.

The report was short.

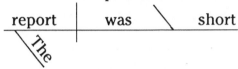

- Diagraming adverbs of degree: The adverb of degree tells you about the adjective. Place it under the adjective on a slanted line.

  The pie was very hot.

  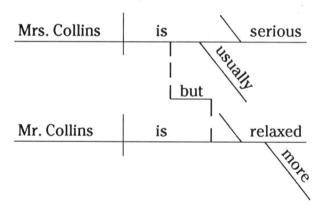

- Diagraming compound sentences: A compound sentence has two complete thoughts. Therefore, each sentence has its own base line. Join the two sentences together with a dotted line to show that they are connected.

  Mrs. Collins is usually serious, but Mr. Collins is more relaxed.

Activity J. Diagram these Pattern 5 sentences. Be sure to place the correct words on the base line. Then place the adjectives, adverbs, and prepositional phrases correctly under those words.

1. Mike looks handsome in his new suit.
2. The chocolate pudding tastes good.
3. Dinner was finally ready.
4. Monday was windy, but it was warm outside.
5. William's report was too long.

Lesson Review

Part A.   Find the linking verbs in each sentence. Make a list of these verbs on your paper.

1. The lemon tasted sour.
2. Sue appears friendly.
3. James is very athletic.
4. Grandmother has been active for many years.

Part B.   Find the predicate adjectives in these sentences. List them on your paper.

1. That microcomputer is small but powerful.
2. Today the air feels chilly.
3. Everyone feels good today.
4. Be careful on that ladder!
5. Was my speech too long?

Part C.   The verb in each sentence below is in boldface. Decide whether or not it is a linking verb. Write the correct answer on your paper.

1. **Stay** loyal to your friends.
2. Later I **am going** to the movies.
3. **Taste** this stew for me.
4. **Is** it too salty?
5. No, it **is** just right!

Lesson 2. Pattern 6 Sentences

A Pattern 6 sentence has a subject, a linking verb, and a predicate noun or pronoun.

Pattern 6 Sentences: Subject + Linking Verb + Noun or Pronoun
Examples:

        S   L.V.   P.N.   S   L.V.   P.N.
That building is a school.   Maryanne is a student.

* The predicate noun or pronoun always follows a linking verb. The predicate noun or pronoun renames the subject.

Activity A.   Write these sentences on your paper.   Complete each sentence with a predicate noun or pronoun.

1. In 1789, George Washington became _____ .
2. Aunt Marie is _____ .
3. The highest mountain in the world is _____ .
4. My favorite movie was _____ .
5. The capital of France is _____ .

* Remember that adjectives describe nouns. There may be adjectives before the predicate noun.
  Example:

        S L.V.   Adj.   P.N.
        She is a pretty girl.

In the example above, *pretty* describes girl.

Activity B. Look at the boldfaced adjectives in each of the following sentences. Write the noun or pronoun each adjective is describing.

1. George Washington was the **first** president.
2. My Aunt Marie is a **good** cook.
3. Carol is always **friendly** to me.
4. Ted looks **tired** today.
5. He seems **overworked.**

- The direct object can be a noun or a pronoun. Study the examples below to understand the difference between a direct object and a predicate noun or pronoun.

    S   V   D.O.   S   L.V.   P.N.
Andy has a motorcycle.   Andy is a motorcyclist.

Motorcycle is not another name for Andy.
Motorcyclist is a person who rides a motorcycle. It renames Andy.

Activity C. Look at the boldfaced noun in each sentence. Decide if it is a direct object or a predicate noun. Write your answer on your own paper.

1. James plays **baseball** in the spring.
2. He is the team **captain.**
3. Kenny is the best **catcher** in the league.
4. He also hits the **ball** a mile.
5. Kenny is the leading **hitter** on the team.

• You may add an adverb or a prepositional phrase to answer questions about the linking verb.

> James is **now** the team captain. (When?)
> James is the captain **at our school**. (Where?)

• You may add a prepositional phrase to describe the predicate noun or pronoun.

> Agatha Christie was the author **of many books**.

Activity D. Find the predicate nouns or pronouns in these sentences. List them on your paper. Remember, the predicate noun is not the object of a preposition.

1. Uruguay is a country in South America.
2. The Nile is one of the world's longest rivers.
3. Mars is the closest planet to the Earth.
4. Coffee is a popular beverage in the United States.
5. *Gone With the Wind* was a popular movie in 1939.
6. Andy's favorite movie is still *Star Wars*.
7. Dana has been Anne's best friend for two years.

Activity E. Write five Pattern 6 sentences. Add as many adverbs, adjectives, and prepositional phrases as you want. Label the required parts of the sentence.

Example:

> S   L.V.   P.N.
> Jackie has been Cynthia's best friend for many years.

- A Pattern 6 sentence may be a command or a request.

L.V.   P.N.

Please be my friend.

L.V.   P.N.

Always remain a true friend.

- A Pattern 6 sentence may also be a question.

  Statement: Carol and Don have been good friends.
  Question: Have Carol and Don been good friends?

- A Pattern 6 sentence may have compound parts. You may join two Pattern 6 sentences together with a conjunction.

S   S   L.V.   P.N.

Tea and coffee are popular drinks.

S   L.V. P.N.   P.N.

A nice dessert is cheese and fruit.

S   L.V.   P.N.   S L.V.   P.N.

John Adams was the second president, but he was also a vice-president.

Activity F.   Write these sentences on your paper. Label the subject, the linking verb, and the predicate noun or pronoun.

1. Was Franklin Pierce a U.S. president?
2. Are those trees oak or maple?
3. That small bird is either a wren or a finch.
4. Maryanne has been a student for thirteen years!
5. *The Good Earth* is a movie and a book.
6. Ted is a student and a salesclerk.

Diagraming Pattern 6 Sentences

The predicate noun or pronoun is placed on the base line of the diagram. It is needed to express the complete thought. The predicate noun renames the subject. The line is slanted toward the subject.

Mr. Ware is a Spanish teacher.

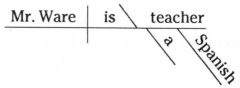

Here is an example of a compound predicate noun.

Ted is a student and a salesclerk.

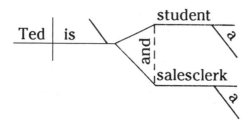

- To diagram a question, change it to a statement. Then draw the diagram.

Is that an oak tree?   That is an oak tree.

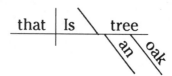

Activity G.   Diagram these Pattern 6 sentences.

1. Who is she?
2. Kim became our class secretary.
3. Sue and Kelly have become good friends.
4. Two popular sports are football and baseball.
5. Paul Dunbar was a poet, and he was a novelist.

Lesson Review

Part A.   Find the linking verb in each of these sentences. Make a list of them on your own paper.

1. *Romeo and Juliet* is a play by William Shakespeare.
2. Edgar Allan Poe was a poet and a story writer.
3. Warsaw is the capital of Poland.
4. Was that a flying saucer?
5. Aunt Marie has been the best cook in our family for years.

Part B.   Write these sentences on your paper. Label the parts.

Examples: S   L.V.   P.N.

          Sudan is a country in Africa.

1. Two popular desserts are pie and cake.
2. The weather feels chilly today.
3. Always be true to your friends.
4. Jupiter is the largest planet in the solar system.
5. The lake is quiet and peaceful in the summer.
6. Is Dan a friend of yours?
7. Who was that?
8. Lima is the capital of Peru.

CHAPTER REVIEW

Part A.   Read each of these sentences. Find the verb and write it on your paper. Decide whether or not it is a linking verb. Write your answer on your own paper.

1. Please taste this stew.
2. Is it too spicy?
3. No, it tastes just right.
4. Are you hungry?
5. No, I have already eaten dinner.
6. I am disappointed.
7. I fixed this stew especially for you.
8. Oh, I am sorry.
9. Do you want a small bowl?
10. Okay, I will eat your stew.

Part B.   Read each of these sentences. Decide whether the boldfaced word is a predicate adjective, a predicate noun, or a predicate pronoun. Write your answers on your own paper.

1. Everyone is **happy** today.
2. Kathleen became a **cheerleader** this year.
3. He is a very good **lawyer**.
4. The capital of Egypt is **Cairo**.
5. Geography is an interesting **subject**.
6. John Steinbeck was a Nobel Prize **winner**.
7. That book is **one** of my favorites.
8. Who is **she**?
9. Of all the seasons, spring is my **favorite**.
10. Sue and Kelly will remain **friends**.

CHAPTER 13

Complex Sentences

Before you study complex sentences, review the meanings of three important terms: *word*, *phrase*, and *clause*.

A *word* is a set of letters that has meaning.

A *phrase* is a group of words that are working together.
    Prepositional Phrase: across the road
    Verb Phrase: has been

A *clause* is a group of words with a subject and a predicate (or verb). There are two kinds of clauses: independent clauses (complete ideas) and dependent clauses (not complete ideas).
    Independent Clause: Rick walked home.
    Dependent Clause: Because he missed the bus

Warm-Up A. Look at these groups of words. Decide which are phrases and which are clauses. Write the answers on your own paper.

1. Over the river.
2. If he leaves.
3. Will have been late.
4. The youngest girl in school.
5. Whoever wants an apple.

- An independent clause is a sentence. It expresses a complete thought.

- A dependent clause has a subject and a verb, but it is not a sentence. There are three kinds of dependent clauses.

	S V S V D.O.
Adverb Clause:	Rick laughed **when he heard the joke**.
	S V S V
Noun Clause:	I remember **what she said**.
	V S S V
Adjective Clause:	There is the lady **that I paid**.

- The dependent clause is introduced by either a subordinating conjunction or a relative pronoun.

    Subordinating conjunctions: *because, if, when, since*
    Relative pronouns: *that, which, who, whoever, what*

Warm-Up B. Read these sentences. Write the dependent clauses on your own paper.

1. That is the boy who just joined the team.
2. The girl who won the contest is in my class.
3. Shelly will study until she finishes.
4. Before the game began, the team exercised.
5. A prize will be given to whoever finished first.

Warm-Up C. Find the word that introduces the dependent clause in each sentence. Write it on your paper.

1. Because Shelly was late, she missed the bus.
2. I will fix dinner if you are hungry.
3. Shelly hoped that the band would win first place.
4. Rick admires the man who coaches his team.
5. What Angela said was not clear to everyone.

- Sentences may be grouped according to purpose or according to pattern.

Warm-Up D. Write each of these sentences on your paper. Label the parts. Write whether the sentence is a statement, question, or command.

Example: S   V   D.O.
            Angela is reading a good book. — Statement

1. Shelly missed the bus.
2. Will Rick hit a home run today?
3. Paint the house green.

- Sentences may also be grouped according to structure. A sentence is either *simple*, *compound*, *complex*, or *compound-complex*.

Simple: One subject and one predicate
                   Sue went to school.

Compound: Two or more ideas joined with a conjunction
                   We looked at new cars, but they were expensive.

Complex: One independent and one dependent clause
                   If the rain stops, we can begin practice.

Compound-Complex: Two independent clauses and at least one
                   dependent clause
                   After I met the girl who lived next door, we became
                   friends; but the next year she moved.

Warm-Up E. Identify the type of each sentence below according to structure. Write your answers on your own paper.

1. They practiced hard and won the game.
2. I'd like to go, but I am too tired.
3. Because we were late, we hurried; but we missed the train anyway.
4. I'll drive if you are too tired.

Lesson 1. The Adverb Clause

A clause is a group of words with a subject and a verb. However, it does not express a complete idea. An adverb clause is used in a sentence exactly like an adverb. It tells something about the verb. Examples:

Adverb:	Rick went home **early**.
Adverb Phrase:	Rick went home **after school**.
Adverb Clause:	Rick went home **when practice was over**.

● Adverbs and adverb clauses also answer the questions, *Where? How much? Why? How often? How soon?*
Examples:

Where?	Angela was happy **wherever she went**.
How much?	Rick gave **as much as he could**.
Why?	Shelly is in the band **because she likes music**.
How often?	Shelly practices **whenever she has time**.
How soon?	**When practice is over**, Rick will go home.

● Remember that a clause must have a subject and a verb.

Activity A. Find the adverb clause in each of these sentences. Write it on your own paper.

1. Rick likes to jog whenever he can.
2. If he gets up early, he jogs in the morning.
3. Rick jogs because he enjoys it.
4. Unless it is raining hard, he jogs every day.

The example below is a simple sentence with a prepositional phrase used as an adverb. The phrase has no subject or verb.

S   V   D.O.   Prep.   N

Shelly has French before lunch.

Adverb Phrase

The example below is a complex sentence with an adverb clause. The subject of the clause is Rick. The verb is arrived.

S   V   S   V

Angela waited an hour before Rick arrived.

Adverb Clause

Activity B. Read each of these sentences carefully. Find the subject and the verb of each clause. Decide whether it is a simple sentence or a complex sentence. Write the answers on your paper.
Examples:

S   V   S   V

Complex: The team was behind until Rick hit a home run.

S   V

Simple: Practice lasted until noon.

1. Every afternoon the baseball team practiced.
2. When practice is over, the players are tired.
3. The team begins with warm-up exercises.
4. If they don't warm up well, injuries are likely.
5. Sometimes the team practices on Saturdays.
6. When it rains, the team can't practice.
7. Baseball is not usually played in the rain.

- An adverb clause may also answer questions about another adverb. These clauses are adverbs of degree. They answer questions like *How much?* or *How far?*

     S   V   D.O.   S   V

  Rick hits the ball farther **than anyone can**.

  The adverb clause tells *how much* farther Rick can hit the ball.

- Sometimes part of the clause is missing. We say the missing part is "understood."

     S   V   D.O.   S

  Rick hits the ball farther **than anyone**.

  In the incomplete clause, the verb is missing. The verb is "understood" to be *can hit*.

- An adverb clause may also answer questions about an adjective. These clauses are also adverbs of degree. Sometimes part of the clause is also understood.

  Examples:

  Complete Clause: Sam is taller **than the others are**.

  Incomplete Clause: Sam is taller **than the others**.

  The adverb clause tells *how much* taller Sam is.

Activity C. Write these sentences on your paper. Underline the adverb clauses.

1. My dog can bark louder than any other dog.
2. Shelly practices longer than anyone else does.
3. Is Angela taller than Sue?
4. Rick jogged longer than the others.
5. Charlotte is as happy as she can be!

Lesson Review

Part A.   Write these sentences on your paper.   Underline the dependent clauses.

1. Sue has been deaf since she was born.
2. Because Angela became Sue's friend, she learned sign language.
3. Anyone can learn sign language if he tries.
4. Sometimes sign language is easier than English is.
5. Angela uses sign language when she is with Sue.

Part B.   Write each sentence on your paper. Draw one line under the subject in each clause. Draw two lines under the verb in each clause. Write any "understood" words in parentheses.

1. We will go to the beach when summer arrives.
2. Cliff bought a motorcycle because he needed transportation.
3. Get some rest if you are tired.
4. No one can run faster than Rick.
5. Rick can hit the ball farther than anyone on the team can.

Part C.   Read these sentences. Look for the subject and verb of each clause. Tell whether each sentence is simple or complex.

Reminder: A simple sentence has one independent clause.
                     A complex sentence also has a dependent clause.

1. Angela and Sue went to the baseball game.
2. They wondered if the team would play.
3. The field was wet because of the rain.
4. They smiled when they saw the team on the field.
5. Although the field was wet, the game began.

Lesson 2. The Noun Clause

A clause is a group of words with a subject and a verb. A noun clause is used in a sentence exactly like a noun.

Examples:

	S L.V. Adj.
Subject:	**What Shelly said** was not clear.
	S L.V. P.N.
Predicate Noun:	That book is **what I need**.
	S V D.O.
Direct Object:	I remember **what you said**.
	S V D.O. O.P.
Object of Preposition:	Mrs. King fixed dinner for **whoever was hungry**.

- Each noun clause has its own subject and verb. It may have a direct object or a predicate noun. The clause may be any of the six sentence patterns.

Example:

S   L.V.   P.N.
Whoever is ready should begin first.

Whoever is ready names the person that is the subject of the sentence. Because it is a clause, it has its own subject, verb, and predicate adjective.

Activity A.   Read each of these sentences. Find the noun clause and write it on your paper. Then decide what part of the sentence the entire clause is.

1. The teacher said that my answer was wrong.
2. Shelly wondered what Angela would say.
3. Who will be first has not been decided.
4. They argued about who should go first.
5. This is what I want.
6. Ralph knows what the score is.

- The noun clause is introduced in a sentence by a relative pronoun. Some common relative pronouns are listed below.

that	who (subject)
what	whom (object)
whatever	whose (possessive)
whichever	whoever (subject)
	whomever (object)

- The relative pronoun is part of the sentence pattern of the noun clause.
Examples:

D.O.   S   V

I remember **whom you called**.

S   V   D.O.

I remember **who called me**.

P.N.   S   L.V.

I remember **who you are**.

The pronoun *that* and *what* have only one form. They do not change when they are subjects or objects. The pronoun *who* does change, however. You must know what the sentence pattern of the noun clause is before you can decide whether to use *who* or *whom*. *Who* is used as the subject of a verb. *Whom* is used as the object of a verb.

Activity B.   Read these sentences. Decide whether *who* or *whom* should be used in each sentence. Write the sentences correctly on your paper.

1. I know _____ called you. (who, whom)
2. I know _____ you are. (who, whom)
3. I know _____ you saw yesterday. (who, whom)
4. I know _____ you invited to the dance. (who, whom)
5. I know for _____ you bought that gift. (who, whom)

- We often use the relative pronoun *that* to introduce a noun clause. Sometimes we choose to leave it out of the sentence. Either way is correct.
  Examples:
Correct:	Do you think **that** he is nice?
Correct:	Do you think he is nice?

- The other relative pronouns cannot be left out.
  Examples:
Correct:	Did you hear **what** I said?
Incorrect:	Did you hear I said?

Activity C. Write each of these sentences on your paper. Underline the noun clause. Circle the relative pronoun. (The relative pronoun that may have been left out of the sentence. Put it in if it belongs and circle it.)

1. Do you know who found my book?
2. Yes, Shelly found the book you lost.
3. What I need right now is that book!
4. I am offering a reward to whoever finds my book,
5. Do you think Shelly has my book now?

Activity D. The noun clauses in the following sentences are in boldface. Decide what part of the sentence each clause is: the subject, direct object, predicate nominative, or the object of a preposition.
Example: **What I said** was not important. — Subject

1. I have a book for **whoever wants it.**
2. I knew **that I would be late.**
3. Some ice cream is **what I need right now!**
4. **What you see** is **what you get!**
5. Tell me **what the answer is.**

- An appositive explains another noun in the same sentence. An appositive is a noun or a noun clause. Look at each example below. The appositive is in italic. The noun that is explained by the appositive is in boldface.

   My **friend** *Angela* has a dog.

   Honey, *a golden retriever*, belongs to Angela.

   The **idea** *that Honey can talk to her* is silly!

Activity E. Find the appositive in each sentence. List the appositives on your paper. Beside each one write the noun the appositive is explaining.

1. Do you know who wrote this line: "All the world's a stage"?
2. Fred's hope that he would win the race kept him going.
3. People laughed at Columbus's idea that the world was round.
4. The nineteenth constitutional amendment, which gave women the right to vote, changed history.
5. Herbert Hoover, the thirty-first president, was an engineer.
6. Galileo's discovery that the earth revolved around the sun changed scientific thought.
7. A bibliography, which is a list of books, appeared at the end of the report.

Lesson Review

Lesson Review. Write these sentences on your paper. Underline the noun clause. Decide what part of the sentence each clause is: the subject, direct object, predicate nominative, or the object of a preposition.
Example:

Did you hear <u>what she said</u>? Direct Object
Sue knew <u>that she and Angela were friends</u>. Direct Object

1. We went shopping for whatever we needed.
2. I think that you can diagram this sentence.
3. The idea that love conquers all is lofty.
4. A glass of lemonade is what I need.

5. She said she's tired.
6. When the paper is due is not clear.
7. Where he was going was not known.
8. I know where he was going.
9. That map is what he needs.
10. He went on an errand for whoever asked him.
11. People laughed at Tom's belief that he could win the contest.
12. You get what you pay for.
13. Is this what the dog brought home?
14. Cliff forgot where he put his book.
15. Tell me who is coming.
16. How Sue did the job was important.
17. What she will do next no one knows.

Lesson 3. The Adjective Clause

An adjective is a word that describes a noun or pronoun. An adjective clause is used in a sentence exactly like an adjective. Examples:

Adjective: The **middle** girl is my sister.

Adjective Phrase: The girl **in the middle** is my sister.

Adjective Clause: The girl **who is in the middle** is my sister.

- You can express the same idea in all three ways. Each sentence is correct. Notice that the adjective clause follows the noun or pronoun.
  Examples:

  The book **that I gave him** was expensive.
  Are you the one **whom I met at the party**?
  Jim invited Sandy, **who is the prettiest girl in school.**
  The lady **whom I recommended** got the job.

Activity A. Find the adjective clause in each of these sentences. Write it on your own paper.

1. A girl whom I know won first prize in a contest.
2. The look that Shelly gave Ralph was meant to kill!
3. The answer that she gave was wrong.
4. The boy who sits in the first seat is absent.
5. We bought a new refrigerator that is guaranteed for one year.

- An adjective clause is introduced by a relative pronoun. Some common relative pronouns are: *who, whom, whose, which, what,* and *that.*

Activity B. Read these sentences. Find the adjective clause in each one. Write it on your paper and circle the relative pronoun.

1. The band that Shelly belongs to went to Florida.
2. They entered a contest that someone organized for high school bands.
3. The director of the band, whose name is Mr. Smith, was very pleased.
4. The band that he had trained performed very well.
5. Mr. Smith hoped the band that he directed would win first place.

Activity C. In each of the sentences below, an adjective is in boldface. Rewrite the sentence. Change the adjective to an adjective clause. Example:

> **Shelly's** band went to Florida.
> The band **that Shelly belongs to** went to Florida.

1. An **old** bus took the band to Florida.
2. The band had a **wonderful** trip.
3. They stayed in a **small** hotel.
4. Everyone enjoyed the **warm** weather.
5. They all looked forward to an **exciting** contest.

Lesson Review

Part A.   Write these sentences on your paper. Underline the adjective clauses. Then write the noun or pronoun each is describing. Example:

   Spring is the season <u>that I like best</u>.— season

1. Please get potato chips that come in a box.
2. Did you know the people who gave the party?
3. Mike is the one who plays right field.
4. The man who drove the bus was very nice.
5. The dress that Sue wore to the party was blue.
6. The girl who was in line behind me bought the last tickets.
7. The man who lived next door moved to Florida.
8. Sue's favorite actor was the one who starred in that movie.
9. Rick read a book that was about the Civil War.
10. We rented a new apartment that had three bedrooms.

Part B.   Read each of these sentences carefully. Decide whether it is simple, compound, or complex. Write your answers on your own paper.

1. I'd like to help you; however, I am too busy.
2. Do you know what Willie said?
3. I think that I've seen that movie before.
4. The person in the middle of the line is my brother Willie.
5. Cliff said he was hungry.

Lesson 4. Complex and Compound-Complex Sentences

A compound sentence has two independent clauses.
Example:

> **I would drive**, but **I am too tired**.

A complex sentence has one independent clause and one dependent clause.
Example:

> **I will drive** if you are tired.

A compound-complex sentence has two independent clauses and one or more dependent clauses.
Example:

> **I will drive** if you are too tired, but **it is your decision**.

Activity A. Read each of these sentences carefully. Find the independent and dependent clauses. Decide whether the sentence is compound, complex, or compound-complex.

1. After she graduated, Shelly hopes to find a summer job.
2. She asked Ralph about a job in Mr. Jackson's store, but he said Mr. Jackson was not hiring.
3. Shelly was discouraged, but she kept on looking.
4. Shelly knows there is a job for her somewhere!
5. Shelly is a girl who doesn't give up easily, and she will look until she finds a job.

- When you want to know how a sentence is constructed, you analyze it. To analyze means to break something down into its parts. You must analyze a sentence to find out whether it is compound, complex, or compound-complex.

- A complex sentence may have more than one dependent clause. Example:

Adjective Clause

Richard Wright, **who was born on a plantation**, worked as a dishwasher **before he became the author of *Native Son***.

Adverb Clause

Activity B.   Answer these questions about the sentence shown below.

Richard Wright, who was born on a plantation, worked as a dishwasher before he became the author of *Native Son*.

1. What is the independent clause in the sentence?
2. What is the subject of the independent clause?
3. What is the verb of the independent clause?
4. Is the verb transitive or intransitive?
5. What are the parts of speech of the words in the phrase *as a dishwasher*?
6. What noun is the adjective clause describing?
7. What question does the adverb clause answer?
8. What is the subject and the verb of the adjective clause?
9. What is the subject and the verb of the adverb clause?
10. There are three verbs (or verb phrases) in the sentence. Which one is a linking verb? What word completes the thought in that clause?

- The same idea may be expressed in different kinds of sentences.

Compound: Ralph is a student, but he also has a part-time job.

Complex: Ralph, who is a student, also has a part-time job.

Compound-Complex: Ralph is a student, but he is also a person who has a part-time job.

Activity C.   Look at the three examples above. Read these questions. Answer them on your paper.

1. Which sentence expresses the idea best?
2. What is the independent clause in the second example?
3. What kind of dependent clause is *who is a student* in the second example? Is it a noun, adjective, or adverb clause?

Activity D.   Rewrite each of these sentences or pairs of sentences. Then, decide what kind of sentence each one is.
Example: Ralph needs a map, and here it is.
               Here is the map that Ralph needs.
                              (or)
               The map that Ralph needs is here.

1. Summer has arrived, and we will go to the beach.
2. American University is in Washington, D.C., and Colleen wants to go there.
3. Graduation will be in June. Willie and Cliff will go to see the girls graduate.
4. The fish are biting, and we will go to the lake.

Activity E.   Read each of the sentences below. Find the independent and dependent clauses. Decide whether each sentence is complex or compound-complex.
Example:

If Rick gets a scholarship, he knows that he can go to college.

Step 1. The independent clause is *he knows that he can go to college.*

Step 2. There is a noun clause which is the direct object of the independent clause, *that he can go to college.*

Step 3. *If Rick gets a scholarship* is an adverb clause.

Step 4. This is a compound-complex sentence.

Step 5. These are the sentence patterns of each clause:
    S   V   D.O.   S   V   D.O.
If Rick gets a scholarship, he knows (that he can go to college)
    S   V   Prep. Phrase
that he can go to college.

1. Mr. and Mrs. King play golf when the weather is warm.
2. Mr. King hits the ball farther than Mrs. King can, but he doesn't putt well.
3. "A new putter is what I need."
4. Mrs. King, whose clubs are old, plays golf very well.
5. Both of them know that new clubs would really help!

• Direct and indirect quotations are noun clauses.
  Examples:

          S   V   Direct Object
  Mrs. King said, "**I enjoyed our golf game**."

          S   V   Direct Object
  Mrs. King said **that she enjoyed the golf game**.

Activity F.   Change each of these indirect quotations to direct quotations. Punctuate your quotation properly.

1. Mr. King told Mrs. King that he wants a new putter.
2. He reminded her that his birthday was in June.
3. She told him that she would buy him a putter.
4. Mr. King said that he wanted to play golf again soon.
5. Mr. King said that he would win next time!

Lesson Review

Lesson Review.   Analyze each of these sentences. Decide whether it is simple, compound, complex, or compound-complex. Write your answers on your paper.

1. Mrs. King planned a party for Shelly because she was graduating from high school.
2. She invited Angela, Sue, Cliff, and Rick.
3. She told Mr. King that she wanted to buy Shelly a car, but he said it was too expensive.
4. "Shelly has a part-time job, and she can save her money for a car."
5. "Buy her a watch instead," Mr. King said.

CHAPTER REVIEW

Part A. A clause always has a subject and a verb. Look at these groups of words. Which are clauses? Which are phrases? Write the answers on your paper.

1. Who is coming
2. to the party
3. for Shelly?
4. Mrs. King is planning a party
5. because Shelly is graduating
6. from high school.
7. It is sad to leave good friends
8. after so many years

Part B. The dependent clauses in these sentences are in boldface. You must decide whether each clause is an adjective, adverb, or a noun. Write your answers on your paper.

1. The person **who is planning the party for Shelly** is her mother, but Mr. King has said **that he will help**.
2. Ralph, **who has already graduated**, has gotten Shelly a present **that he purchased at Mr. Jackson's store**.
3. The party will be held **after the graduation exercises are over**.
4. Mrs. King has planned a surprise for **whichever guest arrives first**.
5. **Whoever it is** will be surprised.
6. **Because the party is for Shelly**, the guests will not expect a gift.
7. Mrs. King will prepare plenty of food **because she knows that everyone will be hungry**.

Part C.   Read the sentence below. Then follow the directions and answer the questions. Write your answers on your paper.

The gift that Mrs. King bought for the first guest is a record album.

1. Find the independent clause in the sentence. Write it on your paper.
2. Label the parts of the independent clause.
3. Write the dependent clause on your paper.
4. Label the parts of the dependent clause.
5. Is the dependent clause an adjective, an adverb, or a noun?
6. What kind of sentence is it? Is it compound, complex, or compound-complex?
7. What is the purpose of the sentence? Is it a statement, a question, or a command?

Part D.   Read each of these sentences carefully. Then decide whether it is simple, compound, complex, or compound-complex. Write the answers on your own paper.

1. Here is a riddle.
2. What has a tongue, but it does not talk?
3. You tie them up when you go for a walk.
4. I'm sure that you know the answer to the riddle, and I want you to write the answer on your paper beside the number 5.
5. Write the answer to the riddle on your paper.

CHAPTER 14

The Verbal
and the Verbal Phrase

A *verbal* is a verb form that is used as a noun or an adjective in a sentence. The three kinds of verbals are *infinitives*, *gerunds*, and *participles*.

* An *infinitive* is a verb form made up of the word *to* plus a verb. It is usually used as a noun, but it may be used as an adjective or adverb.
    Noun: I like to **swim**.
    Adverb: He practices **to win**.
    Adjective: We had lots of food **to eat**.

* A *gerund* is a verb form that ends in *-ing* and is used as a noun.
    Subject: **Swimming** is good exercise.
    Direct Object: We enjoy **swimming**.

- A *participle* is a verb form that is used as an adjective. It describes a noun or a pronoun. There are present and past participles.

  The doll is **lost**. (Past participle: *lost* describes *doll*)
  The **barking** dog scared the stranger. (Present participle: *barking* describes *dog*)

Warm-Up A. Find the verbals in these sentences. List them on your paper.

1. The smiling child was opening presents.
2. Speed is important in running.
3. Jack likes to read.
4. The new magazine was torn.
5. They decided to buy a new house.

- Because an infinitive, a gerund, and a participle are verbs, they may have complements. They may also have adverbs.

  Infinitive Phrase: He hoped **to win the contest**.
  Gerund Phrase: **Cooking dinner** was fun.
  Participle Phrase: We saw Louis **walking down the street**.

Warm-Up B. Find the verbal phrases in these sentences. List them on your paper. Identify the kind of verbal each phrase is.
Example: Louis plans to leave early. — Infinitive phrase

1. Barbara hoped to find a job.
2. After winning the contest, the band celebrated.
3. Their celebrating lasted a long time.
4. To be a good musician takes much practice.
5. In Hanover, Bobby went to play baseball.
6. Winning the games was important to Bobby.
7. He hoped to win a scholarship.

Lesson 1. Infinitives and Infinitive Phrases

An infinitive is *to* + a verb. An infinitive is usually in the present tense. It can also be in the present perfect tense (*to* + *have* + a verb). Examples:

> Nate and Louis decided **to go** to the lake.
> Their plan was **to leave** early.
> They hoped **to catch** many fish.
> They decided **to be gone** by six o'clock.
> They hoped **to have caught** ten fish by noon.

Activity A.   Find the infinitives in these sentences. List them on your own paper.

1. Nate found someone with a small boat that they wanted to use.
2. Nate and Louis really like to fish.
3. They planned to catch enough fish for dinner.
4. Mrs. Agnello agreed to fry the fish.
5. She also decided to make cole slaw and french fries.
6. Nate and Louis were on the lake by seven o'clock, ready to make their first cast.

• Be sure that you do not confuse infinitives with prepositional phrases. An infinitive is *to* + a verb. A prepositional phrase is *to* + a noun.

Infinitives:
$$\overset{\text{V}}{}$$
The boys like **to fish**.
(This includes a verb.)

Prepositional Phrases: They went **to the lake**.
(This has no verb.)

Activity B. Look at the boldfaced phrases. Write them on your paper in order. Identify each phrase as an infinitive or a prepositional phrase.

Example: They went **to the lake to fish**.

           to the lake   — Prepositional Phrase
           to fish— Infinitive

1. When Nate and Louis got **to the lake**, they saw other people ready **to fish**.
2. They carried their equipment **to the boat**.
3. Soon they were ready **to begin**.
4. "I will try **to catch** the first fish," Louis said.
5. "Do you really hope **to beat** the champion?" Nate said **to Louis**.
6. "I hope **to have caught** at least one big one by ten o'clock," said Louis.
7. They said hello **to the other boaters**.
8. "Look!" Nate pointed **to another boat**.
9. "That man just started **to reel** in his line."
10. "He will need a big pan **to fry** that fish!"

- Remember that an infinitive is a verb, but it may be used as a noun, an adverb, or an adjective in a sentence. You must look at the sentence pattern to figure out how an infinitive is used in a sentence. Examples:

              D.O.
Louis wants **to catch** a big fish. (What does Louis want?)

                       Adverb
He will need a big pan **to fry** his fish. (Why does he need a big pan?)

                    Adjective
Nate had plenty of bait **to use**. (What kind of bait does Nate have?)

Activity C. The infinitives in the sentences below are in boldface. Write them on your paper. Decide whether each infinitive is a noun, an adverb, or an adjective. Remember that subjects, predicate nouns, direct objects, and objects of prepositions are nouns.

1. **To catch** a big fish was Louis' ambition.
2. His greatest hope was **to catch** a big fish.
3. After an hour, they decided **to move** to another spot.
4. Their attempts **to catch** a fish were unsuccessful.
5. They tried and tried **to catch** some fish.
6. These fish are hard **to catch**.
7. "A fish would be fun **to catch!**"
8. "Hey! I am about **to catch** a fish!"

An *infinitive phrase* is an infinitive plus any adverb, adverb phrase, or complement it may have.

• An infinitive is a verb form. It may have an adverb or adverb phrase to answer questions about its action.
　Example:　　　**To leave early** was the plan.
　　　　　To leave is an infinitive. It is the subject.
　　　　　Early is an adverb. It answers the question *When?*

• An infinitive may also have a complement. It may have a direct object or a predicate noun.
　Examples:　　　We wanted **to join the club**.
　　　　　Club is the direct object of the infinitive.

　　　　　He wanted **to be the president**.
　　　　　President is the predicate noun.
　　　　　The infinitive *to be* is a linking verb.

- The infinitive may also have a predicate adjective.

Example: We wanted the dinner **to taste good**.

Good is a predicate adjective. *To taste* is a linking verb.
The infinitive *to taste* is an objective complement.

Activity D.   Find the infinitive phrase in each sentence and write it on your own paper.

Examples: INF.   D.O.
                    I am about **to catch a fish**!
                              INF.   D.O. Adv. Phrase
                    Louis wanted **to reel it into the boat**.

Into the boat is a prepositional phrase. It is used as an adverb. It answers the question *Where?*

1. Louis began to reel the fish into the boat.
2. The fish started to fight hard.
3. The fish struggled to get free from the hook.
4. Louis was about to bring it into the boat.
5. Nate got a net to help him.
6. To land that fish was their goal.

- Sometimes the preposition *to* is missing from the infinitive.
  Example:
              "Don't make me **laugh**," shouted Nate.

Activity E.   Find the verb of each sentence. Then find the infinitive and write it on your paper.

1. Will you let me help you?
2. They heard the other boaters cheer for Louis.
3. "Let me see the fish," they all said.
4. They watched Louis hold his fish high in the air.
5. Their attention made Louis smile.

Activity F.   Find the infinitives in these sentences. List them on your paper. After each infinitive, write how it is used in the sentence.

1. Nate's turn to catch a fish came soon.
2. He began to reel his fish to the boat.
3. The fish tried to get free.
4. It seemed to pull hard.
5. To catch a fish is not easy.

Lesson Review

Lesson Review.   Read each of these sentences. Find the infinitive phrase. Write it on your own paper.
Example: It seemed to pull hard.   to pull hard

1. Nate and Louis wanted to be home by dark.
2. They decided to stop at six o'clock.
3. Nate began to count the fish.
4. They had hoped to catch many fish.
5. To catch enough fish for dinner had been their goal.
6. "How many fish are big enough to eat?" asked Louis.
7. "We have enough to feed your family and mine," answered Nate.
8. "Mom will need a big pan to fry this one," Louis said.
9. "Let's get ready to go home," Nate said.
10. They were both ready to leave. It had been a good day.

Lesson 2. Gerunds and Gerund Phrases

A *gerund* is a verb that ends in *-ing.* It is always used as a noun. We use gerunds in sentences in the same ways that we use nouns.

Subject: **Drinking** and **driving** do not mix.

Direct Object: The dog began **barking**.

Predicate Noun: My favorite sport is **swimming**.

Object of a Preposition: The student got in trouble for **cheating**.

Appositive: Nate enjoys two things: **fishing** and **riding** his motorcycle.

Activity A.   Find the gerund in each sentence. Write it on your own paper.

1. Riding a motorcycle is fun.
2. I like jogging better.
3. My favorite activity is playing my trumpet.
4. I get in trouble for cheating.

A *gerund phrase* is a gerund plus any adjective, adverb, prepositional phrase, or complement it may have.

- A gerund is a verb form. We use it in a sentence as if it were a noun. A noun may have an adjective that describes it.
  Example: I get in trouble for loud **talking**.
                    Loud describes the gerund **talking**.

- A gerund may also have an adverb or adverb phrase.
  Example:
  > I like **jogging** in the morning.

  In the morning tells us WHEN Bobby likes **jogging**.

- Because a gerund is a verb, it may have complements.
  Example:

  > Gerund   D.O.
  >
  > **Riding** a motorcycle is fun.

  Motorcycle is the direct object of the gerund **riding**.

Activity B.   Find the gerund phrase in each of these sentences. Write it on your paper. Identify the part the gerund plays in the sentence.
Example:
> **Getting ready for school** is the worst part of the day.
>
>   Getting ready for school — Subject

1. Bobby watched the running of the Boston Marathon on television.
2. Winning that race was one of his dreams.
3. He began thinking about it when he was very young.
4. He got an idea for having his own marathon in Hanover.
5. He began finding joggers.
6. Setting up the race was easy.
7. Bobby enjoys two things: running and winning!

- Don't confuse progressive verbs with gerunds.
  Example:
  Verb Phrase: Bobby **was running** early every day.
  Gerund: Bobby likes **running** every day.

Lesson Review

Lesson Review.   Read these sentences. Find the gerunds or gerund phrases. List them on your own paper.
Example:

My hobby is **collecting stamps**.
collecting stamps

1. Flying an airplane seems exciting.
2. Reading books is a way to relax.
3. We enjoyed swimming in the lake.
4. An architect earns his salary by planning buildings.
5. My dog always gets in trouble for chasing cats.
6. The singing and dancing were good in that play.
7. I like cooking, but not cleaning up.
8. Finding gerunds is easy.
9. Locating a needle in a haystack is usually difficult.
10. A farmer earns money by growing food.
11. Knowing you has been my pleasure.
12. Some people like weeding their gardens.
13. Planning our vacation was fun.
14. His favorite sport is fishing for trout.
15. Dana's hobby is reading.

Lesson 3. Participles and Participial Phrases

A *participle* is another verb form. Participles are used in sentences as adjectives. We also use them as part of a verb phrase.

Examples:
Verb Phrase: The deer **was running** through the woods.
Participle: The **running** deer was beautiful.

Activity A.   Look at the boldfaced words. Decide whether they are part of the verb phrase or whether they are participles.
Example:

The **barking** dog scared the child.   Adjective
The dog was **barking** at the child.   Verb phrase

1. Your cold is probably **catching**.
2. We are **leaving** early in the morning.
3. We will be **catching** the train.
4. The girl came **running** to the train.
5. The **howling** wind kept us awake all night.
6. The wind was **howling** all night.

• A *participial phrase* is a participle plus an adverb or an adverb phrase. It must be next to the noun or pronoun it is describing.

Examples:
Running at full speed, she caught the bus.

The participial phrase, *running at full speed*, describes *she*.

- The participle may also be in the past tense.

     Potato chips are the only snack **needed for the party**.
     Needed for the party describes *snack*.

Activity B.   Write these sentences on your paper. Underline each participial phrase. Draw a line to the noun or pronoun it is describing.

1. Howling wildly, the wind frightened the child.
2. Dana lent her book to the girl sitting in the first row.
3. Expecting the worst, Louis was pleasantly surprised with his grade.
4. The keys locked inside the car were of little use.
5. Reading her book intently, Mrs. Agnello did not hear Louis enter the room.
6. Mr. Agnello mailed the letter addressed to the bank.
7. Recommended by his teachers, Bobby was offered a scholarship.
8. Dinner cooked by Dana was a special treat for Mrs. Agnello.
9. To Barbara, looking from the top of the building, the people looked like ants.

Activity C.   Find the participles and participial phrases in these sentences. Write each one on your paper. Then, write the word that it describes.

Example: **Running at full speed**, the girl caught the bus.
             Running at full speed — girl

1. Walking to school, we passed a new apartment building.
2. Speaking in front of the class, Bobby got nervous.
3. Sodas are the only thing needed for the party.
4. Lost kittens are pitiful.
5. Swimming at the beach, we were frightened by a shark.

Activity D.   List five verbals in these sentences. Then identify each one. It will be a participle, gerund, or an infinitive.

1. Fishing is something that we like to do.
2. The singing waiters brought our food to us.
3. Finding verbals is not hard to do.

Lesson Review

Lesson Review.   Read each of these sentences. Find the participle or the participial phrases. Write them on your paper.

1. We could see the boy running around the track.
2. The old man found his lost dog.
3. Rowing rapidly, we soon crossed the river.
4. The broken bike could not be fixed.
5. Standing on the corner, we watched the cars go by.
6. Arriving early, we were first in line for tickets.

CHAPTER REVIEW

Part A.   Find the verbals in these sentences. List them on your paper. Identify each one as either an infinitive, a gerund, or a participle.

1. To Dana, graduating from high school was an exciting event.
2. Louis went to the graduation to see Dana.
3. Smiling from the stage, Sue received her diploma.
4. Bobby, walking across the stage, almost tripped.
5. "I am a little bit sorry to leave good old Wilson High School," said Barbara.
6. "It's a good excuse to have a party," Nate laughed.

Part B.   Find the verbal phrases in these sentences. List each one on your paper. Identify each one as either an infinitive, a gerund, or a participial phrase.

1. Standing in front of the school for a last look, the girls had tears in their eyes.
2. "Graduating from high school is something that you will always remember," said Mrs. Agnello.
3. As they drove away, Sue turned to catch a last look at her school.
4. Shutting her eyes, Sue thought that she would always remember the good friends that she had made.
5. They all met at Dana's house to celebrate the graduation.

INDEX

A

D

E

G

Y